PLATINUM

THE METAL THAT COULD
MAKE YOU RICH IN THE 1990's

JAMES E. RYAN

Northwest Silver Press
Bellevue, Washington

Cover design by Weathers and Associates
Typesetting and production by Anne and Merle Dowd

Library of Congress Catalog Card No.   90-060927

ISBN 0-9610202-2-9

Contents

List of Tables and Charts

This book is dedicated to the
serious investor who is desirous of
preserving the purchasing power of his
capital and/or making money in the
decade ahead...a time of paradox...of
recession, followed by unprecedented
prosperity—with both periods accom-
panied by raging inflation.

Preface

Platinum, like gold and silver, long dormant after a spectacular price rise to over U.S. $1000 per ounce back in 1980, has acquired a renewed sheen.

This time the platinum price breakout is propelled by an ongoing shortfall and shortage that is compounded by not only specific economic and demand factors that were not present then, but by geopolitical factors as well.

The latter situation; a total economic embargo of South Africa, by the U.S. could have an even more explosive effect on its price which could critically impact your quality of life.

Much has been written about platinum, but yet, there is a strange lack of knowledge about it even on the part of the so called sophisticated investor.

For those, this book will attempt to address that, and in addition, to what is happening to it, why, and how to capitalize on what may be the largest move ever in the price of this noble metal.

James E. Ryan

Acknowledgments

All I have done here is collate the good work and research of others before me in presenting this volume.

My thanks go out to those at the U.S. Bureau of Mines, The Platinum Guild, Int., The Republic of South Africa Department of Minerals and Energy Affairs, Johnson Matthey, the Chamber of Mines of South Africa, Energy, Mines and Resources Canada and the Carnagie Endowment for International Peace. Their information proved invaluable. The conclusions reached, however, are solely those of the author and not to be construed in any way to be those of the above.

My appreciation and thanks also deservidly go to my family for their patience, consideration and understanding during the many days and hours I spent away from them in my study writing this book.

James E. Ryan

Foreword

To me, investing in platinum is indeed a money-making opportunity which is also prudent...even necessary. It's prudent because, like gold, platinum has become universally recognized as a repository of value. It, too, can be likened to an "insurance of last resort." While most insurance has no value unless the insured event occurs, platinum will always maintain an intrinsic value. That is why owning this metal provides a proper balance and diversity to your other holdings.

Lawrence A. Krause, CFP
Lawrence A. Krause & Associates, Inc.

*Lawrence A. Krause & Associates, Inc., headquartered in San Francisco, CA, is one of the leading investment advisory firms in the U.S.

Introduction

This book is about platinum, a gray-white precious metal, of which only 85 tonnes are produced each year, of which the United States has almost none—but needs much more for its industrial needs.

It's also about South Africa, the country that now owns 90 percent of the world's reserves of platinum and why the U.S. is waging an economic war against them; a war that is getting hotter and that could develop quickly into an armed conflict.

This book reveals too, for the first time, the existence of an invasion plan, details of which spell out exactly the numbers of ships, aircraft, combat troops necessary and even the number of casualties that the United Nation's Forces invading South Africa could expect to suffer in its war over platinum!

This book discloses also who now is buying up most of the world's platinum production and why. Then you are taken analytically step by step through the various platinum investment options available that might make you rich.

The book then concludes with an impartial evaluation of all the pros and cons that could have a bearing on platinum's price.

Lastly, and finally, the unfinished saga of cold fusion is examined in light of its relationship to platinum now and its probable effect on platinum's future.

1

The Platinum Predicament Facing the U.S.

"U.S. dependency on platinum from South Africa is so great that if the United States was ever cut off from its supply, it would have to restructure its industry. It's an immediate problem." T.S. Ary, Director, U.S. Bureau of Mines, said at a meeting of the American Mining Congress awhile back.

With U.S. industry drawing 85 to 90 percent of its platinum from South Africa and with no safe alternative supply source; Mr. Ary further stated that if supplies were cut off, such an emergency might force the United States consumer to forget some of the "niceties of life!"

Many of the industry representatives and mining analysts at that meeting and at other similar meetings have concurred with this analysis.

1

Table A

Platinum Supply and Demand: Western World

Supply	1979	1980	1981	1982
South Africa	2,180	2,320	1,800	1,960
Canada	130	130	130	120
Others	30	30	30	30
	2,340	2,480	1,960	2,110
USSR Sales	460	340	370	380
TOTAL SUPPLY	**2,800**	**2,820**	**2,330**	**2,490**
Demand by Region				
Western Europe	430	290	420	330
Japan	920	940	1,150	1,050
North America	1,340	980	700	710
Rest of Western World	160	120	160	230
	2,850	2,330	2,430	2,320
Western Sales to Comecon/China	30	30	30	30
TOTAL DEMAND	**2,880**	**2,360**	**2,460**	**2,350**
Movements in Stocks	(80)	460	(130)	140
	2,800	2,820	2,330	2,490

Our supply figures are estimates of sales by the mines of primary platinum. The demand estimates shown in this table are net figures, demand in each sector being total purchases by consumers less any sales back to the market. Thus, the annual totals represent the amount of primary metal that is acquired by consumers in any particular year.

1983	1984	1985	1986	1987	1988
2,070	2,280	2,340	2,350	2,520	2,560
80	150	150	150	140	145
40	40	40	40	40	95
2,190	2,470	2,530	2,540	2,700	2,800
290	250	230	290	400	400
2,480	**2,720**	**2,760**	**2,830**	**3,100**	**3,200**
330	400	400	470	560	545
950	1,140	1,250	1,010	1,650	1,915
720	910	1,010	1,190	900	850
180	180	170	170	180	310
2,180	2,630	2,830	2,840	3,290	3,620
20	30	30	40	30	40
2,200	**2,660**	**2,840**	**2,840**	**3,320**	**3,660**
280	60	(100)	(50)	(220)	(460)
2,480	2,720	2,760	2,830	3,100	**3,200**

Movements in stocks in a given year reflect changes in stocks held by other than primary refiners and final consumers, such as metal in the hands of fabricators, dealers, banks, and individuals. A positive figure indicates an increase in stocks; a negative figure indicates a rundown in stocks.

Courtesy Johnson Matthey

The grim scenario presented is obviously not just undue pessimism on the part of beleagered bureaucrats and industrial users. It is a stark but frank admission that most of our platinum supply could be in jeopardy.

The situation is particularly ominous primarily because South Africa is threatening the U.S. with retaliation if Congress passes an even more severe economic sanctions bill, which is now before both Houses. (See sanctions bill in Appendix A.)

The measure, as it now stands, would not only ban most exports to South Africa from the U.S., but all imports to the U.S. from their country except for platinum group metals.

Although later denied, an unnamed spokesman for the government of South Africa referred to this latest sanctions measure as "an act of economic terrorism" and said that if the legislation was passed, it would leave South Africa with no other option but to restrict the flow of key metals and minerals to the U.S.

Supply Problem Compounded

This threat, along with an already tight supply situation for platinum, would send the price well beyond anything imagined.

Even U.S. $2,000 per ounce is not out of the question according to a U.S. Bureau of Mines special report, which indicates such a price rise would not only be possible but be a swift reaction to the sanctions bill becoming law. Is it no wonder that there is serious industry concern over this matter because we already are experiencing accelerating worldwide consumption of platinum.

Japan alone last year used over 68 of the 90 tonnes of platinum that was produced, and now, in addition to this, we have the sudden opening up of the East-block countries' markets.

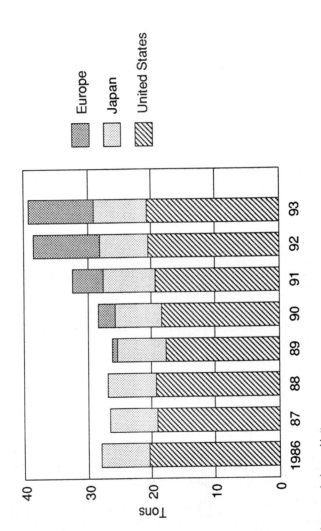

Forecast of Platinum Use in Cars

Europe

Japan

United States

Source: Shearson Lehman Hutton

Plainly and simply, there is not enough platinum to go around, unless new reserves are found and made available and/or consumption is restricted by this price action.

How long has there been a problem? Most experts will agree that the United States was not always dependent on South Africa for platinum because amounts that were needed then came from Canada. Platinum really didn't come into its own and become important to industry until after World War II. Since then, we have had an electronic revolution bringing us T.V. and many other niceties—which now, of course, have become necessities, thus increasing the need for substantial amounts of platinum.

So as it stands now, we cannot exist as the nation we are today and maintain our present standard of living without imports such as platinum.

In a desperate attempt to offset our shortage of platinum, the U.S. Government mandated that a strategic stock pile of one million ounces is to be maintained. That stock pile stands today at only 439,000 ounces. The serious concern on the part of our leaders over this dwindling supply has now put the U.S. in a confrontational position vis-à-vis South Africa.

Positions have hardened since on both sides. Total capitulation—a takeover of the South African government by the African National Congress and total nationalization of the mines is the United States and the black majority position—and this is simply unacceptable to the ruling white minority at this juncture.

If the platinum mines in South Africa are taken forcefully, blood will be let, and many lives will be lost.

2

Why Platinum is in Such Great Demand

Its Many Uses

The name Platinum, although not yet a household word or commonly used in one's everyday vocabulary, is still generally recognized as being something that is valuable, beautiful or having to do with riches.

Its importance, however, in our everyday lives exceeds its recognition. *Platinum now is an integral part of over 20% of all manufactured goods in the Western World.*

Automobile catalysts now consume over 60 percent of world platinum production, and that figure not only

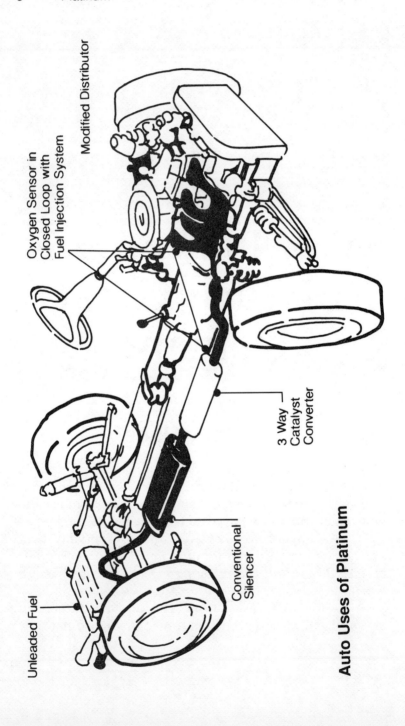

Modified Distributor

Oxygen Sensor in
Closed Loop with
Fuel Injection System

3 Way
Catalyst
Converter

Conventional
Silencer

Unleaded Fuel

Auto Uses of Platinum

could, but will grow dramatically with the opening up of China and the "Iron Curtain" countries of Europe.

Other and important industrial uses of platinum include petroleum refining, chemical production, electronics—including electrical circuits; thermocouples and

Catalytic converters use platinum group metals to reduce harmful automobile emissions.

Proportion of Cars Fitted with Catalysts on the Road - by Region 1983-1998

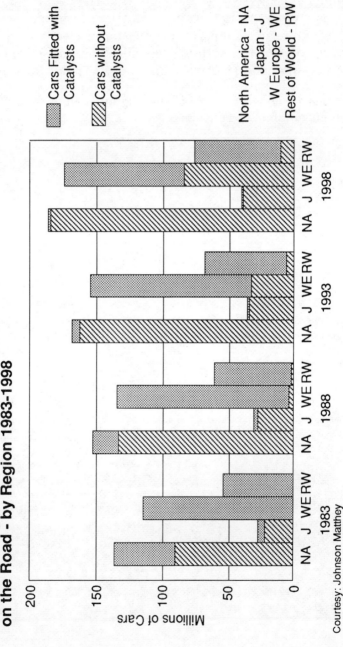

Courtesy: Johnson Matthey

electrical contacts; glass manufacturing and medical uses. These are just the essential uses—and which in most cases, no substitutions are likely or possible. I did not include jewelry, legal tender coins, or investment bullions, but if included, their consumption alone would exceed 28 percent of platinum produced.

Autocatalysts

As previously pointed out, the most important industrial platinum application is for automobile catalytic converters, devices for controlling or lessening contaminants that cause air pollution given off by motor vehicles.

The catalytic converter basically is a canister connected to the exhaust system of the typical automobile. It contains a combination of platinum group metals in the inner honeycomb core that filters the fumes or exhaust gases that are released when the automobile is being operated.

Autocatalysts have proven to be the most effective technology yet developed for reducing pollution from cars, and their use is expanding into Europe and the Far East. At this writing, Johnson Matthey has just announced the opening of a new automobile catalytic converter factory in Belgium that will produce five million units annually, the capacity of which can be doubled later on or as needed. Reuters report, also, that starting February 12, 1990, all new model Volkswagen cars sold in West Germany will be equipped with catalytic converters as standard equipment. Volkswagen has been the largest manufacturer of automobiles in Western Europe for the last five years (15% of all cars sold in Western Europe are made by Volkswagen). Eventually, even motor bikes—which seem to operate in such uncontrolled swarms in cities like Taipei and elsewhere will be required to have these smog reducing devices.

Platinum Demand in the Western World 1988

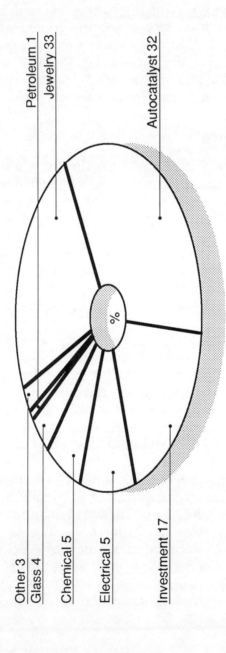

Petroleum 1
Jewelry 33
Autocatalyst 32
%
Other 3
Glass 4
Chemical 5
Electrical 5
Investment 17

Total Demand = 3,620,000 oz (net demand figures for all applications)

Courtesy: Johnson Matthey

The environmental needs and desires of the hundreds of millions of people now just beginning to breathe the air of freedom, after their long containment in the East-block will also be an expanding market for automobiles in the decade ahead. Platinum group metals will have to be shared with them too. Hopefully, substitutes may be found to lesson the pressure on existing supplies by that time.

Possible Platinum Replacements or Substitutes

As of today, there are no substitutes for platinum group metals used in automobile catalytic converters.

Last year the Chairman of Ford Motor Company alluded to his company as having found a new and cheaper

Pure platinum threads used in the production of nitrogen-based fertilizers.

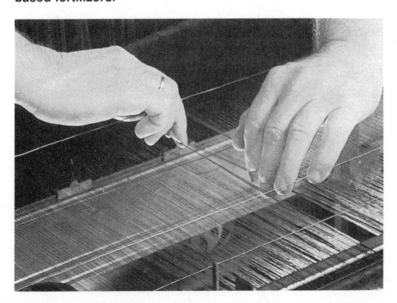

replacement for platinum group metals for catalytic converters. It caused quite a stir in the industry and simultaneously sharply depressed the price of platinum.

The news release came exactly as the price of platinum broke over U.S. $620 per ounce. There never was a follow-up release and/or further details given.

Commodity futures traders had a field day with the

The major use of palladium in electronics is in multi-layer ceramic capacitors (MLCC). The capacitor electrodes of MLCC are made from various palladium-silver compositions. Japanese-made MLCC such as those in the center of this photograph are encapsulated in resin before use in a multitude of electronic devices.

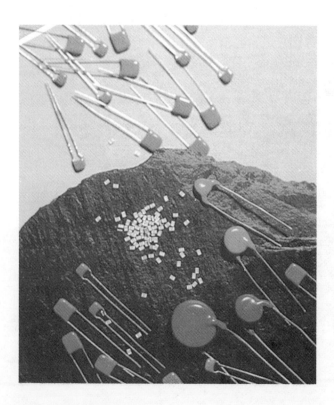

price gyrations that took place, until statements and information came out from other industry sources suggesting that there were *no substitutes*.

The price climbed back up and nothing more has come out on this matter since.

At the time of Ford's statement, the shortfall of platinum was substantial and growing, and the price was at a critical breakout level on the charts.

Some experts read into this that this may have been an outright attempt to affect the market on platinum. Rumors and disinformation like this have been used effectively on countless occasions over the centuries, for financial gain by financiers, companies and governments. There is no reason not to think that it won't continue in spite of laws that prohibit this kind of thing.

So far as substitutes for platinum are concerned, there is presently nothing on the horizon that looks promising.

Chemicals Production and Platinum

The most important area of application in the chemical industry is in the production of nitric acid, essential for fertilizer and explosives manufacture and many other chemical uses.

A platinum-rhodium alloy is used in weaving the gauzes for the catalytic production of nitric acid. A catalytic charge in a modern plant could weigh 85 kilograms, with a current value of $1.75 million, and last through a cycle of three months during which 90,000 tonnes of nitric acid would be produced. Until recently 20 to 30 percent of the platinum alloy gauze could be lost due to attrition and volatization during operation. Today, sophisticated systems for reducing these losses have been developed, generally by using palladium, another platinum group metal.

Since most fertilizers and hence world food production are reliant on the manufacture of nitric acid, the importance of platinum group metals in this process cannot be over exaggerated. Before platinum group metal catalysts existed, bulk production of nitric acid was not practical. Considerable efforts have been made to find base metal alternatives in this process, but they cannot provide continuous production and, therefore, be reliable and cost-competitive.

The Electronics Industry and Platinum

The platinum group metals have been associated with the electrical and electronics industry for almost as long as the metals themselves have been refined and fabricated. For many years their unsurpassed metallurgical properties accounted for their widespread application, particularly in electrical contacts and various electronic systems.

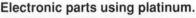

Electronic parts using platinum.

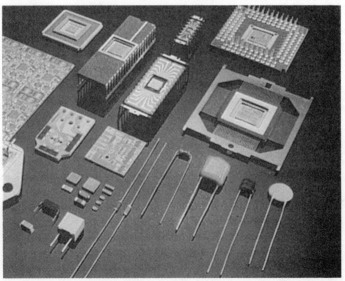

However, the 1950's saw the beginning of the micro-electronic revolution which changed the need for the platinum metals but in no way made them redundant. Instead, it opened up a wide range of new applications. For example, while the need for low-current contacts gradually diminished as electronic switching progressed, reliable and cost-effective materials were required for new micro-electronic devices. High technology generated a new impetus for the platinum metals.

The platinum group metals proved indispensable in the new micro-electronic revolution for several reasons. One of the most important is that a very little platinum goes a very long way. The unsurpassed metallurgical benefits of the platinum group metals can be obtained with only microscopic quantities. Sputtering is a good example of this, where materials are coated by electron bombardment methods with a layer of precious metal, the thickness of which is measured in Angstroms (millionths of a millimeter).

Despite being precious metals, the actual platinum group metal content of micro-electronic components is small and consequently of little value. In the electronics industry the cost of assembly far outweighs the cost of components. Components are, however, made by the billion and to check each one is impossible; reliability is nevertheless paramount if costly rejection of finished assemblies is to be avoided. This is where platinum group metals come into their own; experience has shown that where they are applicable, their performance and reliability are far superior to other metals.

It is therefore not surprising to discover platinum group metals in almost every facet of electronic technology. Examples of major applications in terms of metals consumption are thick film resistors, thick film conductors, multi-layer ceramic capacitors and connectors.

The Glass Industry and Platinum

In this industry the use of platinum metals can be split broadly into two sectors: glass fibre, and other optical and high performance glass. In both cases, the industry has been dependent upon platinum to attain the position it holds today.

Glass fibre is a fairly recent innovation. The fibres, formed as molten glass, are extruded through fine bushings. From the time they were first made, rhodium/platinum alloys have been used to make the bushings. To date there is no viable alternative. Other possible materials are incapable of withstanding the temperatures and severity of operating conditions necessary for continuous production; constant replacement would be required.

While the capital cost of making bushings from platinum is high, it is essential for the production of glass fibre. However, operating costs are low. Less than two percent of platinum is lost from a four kilogram bushing annually. The operating cost of using platinum is currently in the region of $15 per bushing—glass output from a bushing is in the order of 500 tonnes.

In the case of optical and high performance glass, platinum has been used since the early 19th century. For some 100 years technicians have looked unsuccessfully for a substitute. Glass was of poor quality, both in purity and physical form before platinum was used and could be produced in only small amounts thus restricting the size of finished items—in those days almost exclusively lenses.

The availability of high quality glass has allowed immense growth in a wide range of industries such as camera, instrument manufacture, video equipment and television. These uses of high purity, high performance glasses are still expanding, particularly in the electronics field. As with fibre glass, the main cost of using platinum is capital back-up, since metal losses during glass production are negligible.

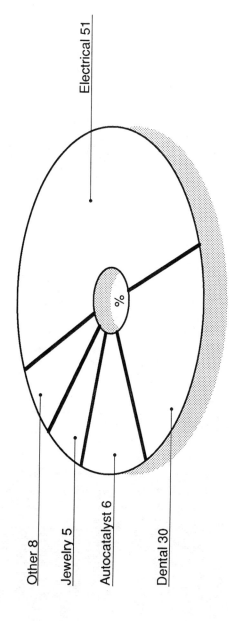

Palladium Demand in the Western World 1988

Electrical 51

Other 8

Jewelry 5

Autocatalyst 6

Dental 30

%

Total Demand = 3,315,000 oz (net demand figures for all applications)

Courtesy: Johnson Matthey

Rhodium   Total Demand= 270,000 oz

Autocatalyst 68%

Glass 4%
Electrical 6%
Chemicals 9%
Other 13%

Ruthenium   Total Demand= 240,000 oz

Electrochemical 43%

Electrical 42%

Other 15%

Iridium   Total Demand= 33,000 oz

Other 44%

Electrochemical 25%

Crucibles 11%
Petroleum 12%
Catalyst 8%

Osmium

The market for the
highly specialised
applications of this
mineral is so thin that
accurate data is
unavailable

Petroleum Refining and Platinum

Platinum is essential to the petroleum refining industry. The platinum metal is used as a reforming catalyst which upgrades distillate-naphthas, recovered from crude oil, into higher octane petroleums. The platinum catalyst allows easier production of higher octane fuels and also leads to a more complete exploitation of the various fractions of crude oil.

While the very large amount of metal installed in refineries throughout the world may add up to some 80 tonnes, purchases of new metal have tended to decline during the past 20 or so years. This has been due to two factors. One is common to all industrial processes, especially

Platinum metals are indispensable in the refining of high octane petroleum fuels.

those using precious metals, and is the result of improved efficiencies. The other is the squeeze in the 1970's by OPEC which halted the profligate use of the world's energy resources. Consequently, the petroleum industry has, to a large extent, been self-financing in platinum needs. There was, however, a small improvement in platinum sales to the industry in 1986.

Platinum's Importance in the Medical Field

Since 1980 the use of palladium as a dependable, cost-effective substitute for gold in dentistry has grown by 75 percent. Last year nearly one million ounces, or 30 percent of total western world demand, was used in dentistry world-wide.

Platinum, in the form of Cisplatin, is the most successful chemotherapeutic agent yet developed for the treatment of certain types of cancer and in particular that of the testes and ovaries. Carboplatin is one of several second generation platinum compounds investigated for use in cancer chemotherapy which gained approval in Canada and the United Kingdom in March 1986 for the treatment of ovarian cancers and small-cell lung cancers. With anti-tumour activity comparable to that of Cisplatin, Carboplatin has the advantage of causing fewer toxic side effects.

Studies show that platinum metals may one day play a role in fighting viral, bacterial and parasitic infections. The metal shows additional promise as an important diagnostic tool, especially for hepatitis and other disorders.

Fuel Cells and Platinum

A new generation of fuel cells generates electricity by combining hydrogen and oxygen to produce water. Fuel cells have been used to provide electric power in space-craft. Extensive research programs are now underway in several countries to establish commercial, terrestrial applications for both centralized and local power generation.

The cell has significant advantages over more conventional methods of power generation: it is "clean" (producing no environmentally offensive contaminates), has high intrinsic electrical efficiencies (40 percent, plus) with good performance both at peak and part loads over a wide range of practical power ratings. By contrast, conventional plants have an efficiency range of 20 to 30 percent depending on rated size and maximum load.

Despite these important advantages, the fuel cell has not made a commercial impact yet because of high capital cost. However, development is actively continuing under private initiative and government-funded programs in the main industrialized countries of the western world.

Japan, whose dense population is extremely sensitive to environmental issues, is a leader in this area of technology. Several private companies in Europe, the USA and Japan are working on the small-scale cells—up to about 10kW—for boats, small vehicles and mining applications.

The potential of fuel cells is almost unlimited, and thus they offer tantalizing opportunities for commercial development.

Jewelry and Platinum

Platinum demand in jewelry manufacturing is now into its sixth year of consecutive growth using well over one million ounces, with Japan the leader in the field. The growth of this section of the market will grow at an even faster pace because of inflation and a boom in consumer spending in Japan.

Much of the increase is tied in with the growth in retail diamond sales. Platinum and diamonds go together.

Diamonds set in rings and chains are big sellers.

Given that there is no end in sight to the current era of prosperity in Japan, there is every prospect of a continuing increase in demand for platinum jewelry in the years ahead.

Fashion-conscious consumers, outside of Japan, are becoming aware of platinum, and these markets are expanding also, with manufacturing burgeoning in Italy, Germany, Hong Kong, Singapore and Thailand. An interesting observation regarding platinum is as the price increases, the demand tends to accelerate.

Investment Demand and Its Effect

As to the outlook for platinum investment products, there is little doubt that the demand for coins and

The physical properties of platinum enable it to be used in unconventional ways. These two rings were made by Niessing in West Germany. The stones are held in position purely by the strength of the platinum.

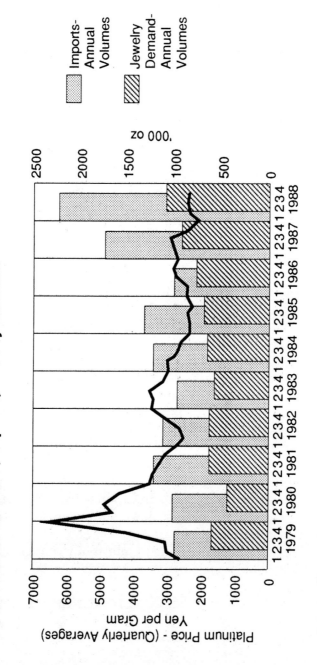

Japan: Platinum Prices, Imports, Jewelry Demand

Courtesy: Johnson Matthey

bullion bars is already having a critical effect on the available supply of platinum.

The platinum coin market was dominated until recently by the Isle of Man Noble. Then Canada and Australia each produced a well accepted legal tender one-ounce platinum coin.

Canada's Maple Leaf and Australia's Koala are already a big success with demand increasing day by day.

Other coins, although not classified as official legal tender coins by their respective governments, are also gaining popularity, with Johnson Matthey's Platinum Dragon leading the way in the Orient.

Coin minting is becoming just another major consumer of platinum that will put additional upward pressure on the price while simultaneously reducing the supply.

Although they haven't appeared yet, there is confirmation that Russia also is coming out with several ruble denominated platinum coins. Their numbers are expected to be limited, and because of this will sell at quite a premium.

Platinum bars in one-, 10-ounce and larger are an important part of the investment market. Also, Japanese consumption still has by far the major impact on this market. As activity increases, platinum bars, not always available, may take up to three months to get delivery due to minimal above ground supplies.

This segment of the market is bound to become more active and widespread as inflation fears impact it—again adding to the existing shortage and pushing the price of platinum higher faster.

The story on the demand for platinum would not be complete without discussing its relationship to the world population explosion.

This "time bomb" keeps on ticking each minute,

each hour and each day, year after year with no end in sight.

All of these people have to be fed and clothed, and industry has to provide for their needs as time goes on. Needless to say, no one has the answer as to how this can be accomplished. T.R. Malthus warned of what is coming in his *An Essay on the Principle of Population* in 1798. The world population then was slightly over one billion. Today it is thought to be over five billion. At the end of this decade who knows, it's almost immaterial.

What of the platinum shortage now? What will industry do? The demand will be compounding. There is no good answer to the platinum crisis any more than there is an answer as to where the additional food will come from to feed the additional billions of people as time goes on.

Rich or poor, the quality of life of everyone will be affected.

Table B

Platinum Demand by Application: Regions
'000 oz

	1979	1980	1981	1982
Japan				
Autocatalyst: gross	200	210	190	170
recovery	(0)	(0)	(0)	(0)
Chemical	10	10	10	10
Electrical	15	15	15	20
Glass	40	40	50	45
Investment: small	0	0	0	0
large	0	160	195	115
Jewellery	590	440	625	620
Petroleum	10	15	15	15
Other	55	50	50	55
TOTALS	920	940	1,150	1,050
North America				
Autocatalyst: gross	670	440	430	455
recovery	(0)	(0)	(0)	(0)
Chemical	130	115	50	80
Electrical	135	145	70	70
Glass	100	50	20	10
Investment	0	0	0	40
Jewellery	15	15	15	15
Petroleum	195	140	55	20
Other	95	75	60	20
TOTALS	1,340	980	700	710
Rest of Western World including Europe				
Autocatalyst: gross	30	30	20	20
recovery	(0)	(0)	(0)	(0)
Chemical	205	135	190	170
Electrical	90	50	100	80
Glass	110	50	30	30
Investment	0	0	0	5
Jewellery	160	105	115	130
Petroleum	(45)	(25)	70	30
Other	40	65	55	95
TOTALS	590	410	580	560

1983	1984	1985	1986	1987	1988
170	170	210	255	310	330
(0)	(0)	(0)	(5)	(15)	(25)
10	15	15	15	15	15
20	30	40	45	45	45
60	75	60	30	45	45
5	15	35	35	60	130
65	150	170	(125)	275	300
560	625	675	740	900	1,060
15	20	15	0	0	0
45	40	30	20	15	15
950	**1,140**	**1,250**	**1,010**	**1,650**	**1,915**
450	635	700	745	690	690
(30)	(45)	(70)	(85)	(100)	(135)
100	100	75	65	55	55
90	95	80	65	65	65
15	30	40	25	25	25
40	30	130	300	85	70
15	15	15	15	15	15
15	15	10	10	15	15
25	35	30	50	50	50
720	**910**	**1,010**	**1,190**	**900**	**850**
25	35	70	140	255	305
(0)	(0)	(0)	(0)	(0)	(0)
135	145	135	115	125	90
65	65	80	70	70	75
30	35	40	35	50	60
45	125	95	115	70	130
140	135	120	95	75	105
(10)	(20)	(10)	10	40	35
80	60	40	60	55	55
510	**580**	**570**	**640**	**740**	**855**

Courtesy Johnson-Matthey

A typical platinum mine in the Bushveld Complex.

3

Who Has All the Platinum?

South Africa

South Africa stands out as the major producer of platinum group metals in the world, followed by Russia, Canada, Australia and the United States.

Of the approximately 90 tonnes produced each year, South Africa accounts for about 89 percent, Russian 7 percent and the other countries for the balance.

Most of South Africa's production comes from the Merensky and UG2 Reefs, the mining done by just a few major mining companies. Although expansion of these operations are continuing, the increase in production has not been able to keep up with burgeoning world-wide demand for platinum.

The Bushveld Complex of South Africa, where

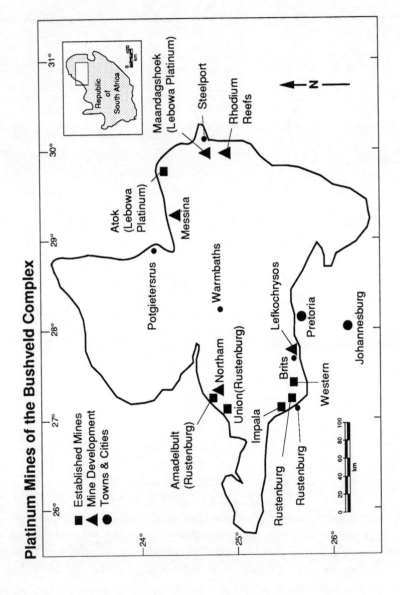

Platinum Mines of the Bushveld Complex

platinum group metals come from, is a large igneous (volcanic) intrusion through the earth's crust which having been tilted and eroded now outcrops to surface around what appears to be the edges of a great geological basin.

However, investigation continues into the genesis of the Bushveld, and quite recently modern vibrosis (seismic) techniques of exploration have thrown new light on to the subterranean structure of the Bushveld.

The Bushveld is divided into an eastern and western lobe with a further northern extension. It is now believed that these three portions are not connected underground as was earlier thought. However, the three sections of the system are believed to have formed at approximately the same period—some 2000 million years ago—and are remarkably similar. Current opinion is that igneous magmas were brought to surface through long vertical cracks in the earth's crust. In each case they then spread outward horizontally, between layered sedimentary rocks of the Transvaal Sequency to reach surface. The intruding magma tilted above it, an oval shaped "roof" of older rocks which today appear as the central filling to the Bushveld complex.

Differential crystallization in the cooling magmas has led to the formation of almost pure mineral layers including two major platinum bearing reefs.

The Merensky Reef has to date been the source of most of South Africa's platinum group metals. Although this Reef in the western Bushveld occurs in a narrow platinum group metal-rich band—25 centimeters wide— bounded by two thin chromite layers, this pattern deteriorates in other areas, resulting in the reef diverging between the chromite bands until it is many meters wide. In these areas, the platinum group metals are generally too dispersed to make mining of this ore a commercial proposition although an upper band is, on occasion, worth extracting.

Geographical Locations of World Platinum Group Metal Reserves

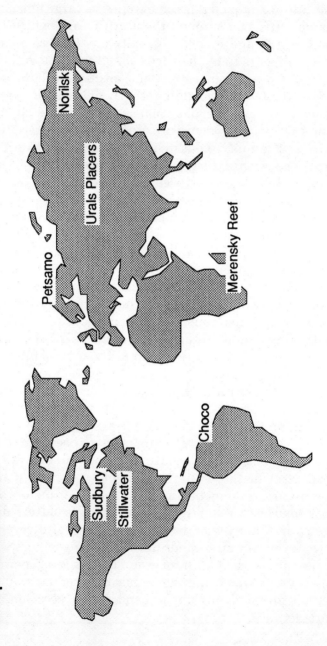

The UG2 Reef, on the other hand, is generally consistent throughout the Bushveld Complex but in the past has been almost impossible to process because of its high chromium content, which created substantial problems in the smelting phase. New mineral processing methods are now rendering the UG2 Reef potentially exploitable.

In the northern extension of the Bushveld, the wide Plat Reef is found but contains lower platinum group metal grades then the Merensky Reef. Although exploited in the past, the Plat Reef has not been mined recently.

Canada

In the case of problems with South Africa, Canada will become much more important, not only as a source of platinum but from increased exploration activity.

Canadian platinum output now is largely a by-product of nickel mining and consequently varies with the nickel market. INCO and Falconbridge mines produce almost all of Canada's platinum, principally from nickel-copper sulphide deposits around Sudbury, in southern Ontario. Platinum production in 1988 was approximately 155,000 ounces, although a higher output is expected in 1990.

Several new Canadian platinum ventures are under investigation, including two in the Great Lakes region of Ontario.

Their preliminary output is estimated at some 130,000 ounces but this could nearly double Canada's platinum production during the 1990's. Other projects of considerable potential are Boston Bay Mines' Lac des Iles property north of Thunder Bay, also shared by American platinum, Longreach Resources' leases in the Franklin mining district of British Columbia, Nexus Resources' prospects in the Tulameen district and on Vancouver

Table C

Platinum Group Metals: World Production, by Country[1]
(Troy ounces)

Country[2]	1984
Australia, metal content, from domestic nickel ore:[3]	
Palladium	16,815
Platinum	2,122
Canada: Platinum-group metals from nickel ore	348,216
Colombia: Placer platinum	10,106
Ethiopia: Placer platinum[e]	125
Finland:	
Palladium	1,093
Platinum	1,061
Japan, metal recovered from nickel-copper ores:[5]	
Palladium	33,802
Platinum	19,523
South Africa: Platinum-group metals from platinum ore[e 6]	3,500,000
U.S.S.R.: Placer platinum and platinum-group metals recovered from nickel-copper ores	3,700,000
United States: Placer platinum and platinum-group metals from gold-copper ores	14,635
Yugoslavia:[e]	
Palladium	[4] 3,476
Platinum	[4] 386
Zimbabwe:	
Palladium	1,222
Platinum	772
TOTAL	[r] 7,653,354

1985	1986	1987 [p]	1988 [e]
15,304	13,760	[e]15,800	13,200
3,054	3,697	[e]4,200	3,400
337,088	391,917	351,407	[4]368,383
11,650	14,368	20,500	26,200
150	150	150	150
1,125	3,086	2,862	3,000
1,125	3,858	3,860	4,000
43,703	46,699	45,568	38,500
22,216	21,312	24,202	20,900
3,700,000	3,960,000	4,220,000	4,285,000
3,800,000	3,850,000	3,900,000	3,900,000
W	W	W	W
3,300	3,100	[r]3,200	3,200
250	250	[r]95	100
965	1,125	932	1,000
611	836	579	600
7,940,541	**8,314,158**	**8,593,355**	**8,667,633**

U.S. Bureau of Mines

Island and the remote Equinox Resources' site near the Arctic Circle.

Australia

Only small amounts of platinum group metals are mined in Australia, and are principally by-products of Western Mining's nickel operations at Kambalda. In the last two years, some 60 companies have been investigating platinum prospects. Two such projects are the Coronation Hill venture and the alluvial deposits in the Fifield area of New South Wales.

Footnotes to Table C, preceding page

eEstimated. PPreliminary 'Revised. W Withheld to avoid disclosing company proprietary data; not included in "Total."

1Table includes data available through May 2, 1989. Platinum-group metal production by the Federal Republic of Germany, Norway, and the United Kingdom is not included in this table because the production is derived wholly from imported metallurgical products and to include it would result in double counting.

2In addition to the countries listed, China, Indonesia, Papua New Guinea, and the Philippines are believed to produce platinum-group metals, and several other countries may also do so, but output is not reported quantitatively, and there is no reliable basis for the formulation of estimates of output levels. However, a part of this output not specifically reported by country is presumably included in this table credited to Japan. (See footnote 5.)

3Partial figure; excludes platinum-group metals recovered in other countries from nickel ore of Australian origin; however, a part of this output may be credited to Japan. (See footnote 5.)

4Reported figure.

5Japanese figures do not refer to Japanese mine production, but rather represent Japanese smelter-refinery recovery from ores originating in a number of countries; this output cannot be credited to the country of origin because of a lack of data. Countries producing and exporting such ores to Japan include (but are not necessarily limited to) Australia, Canada, Indonesia, Papua New Guinea, and the Philippines. Output from ores of Australian, Indonesian, Papua New Guinean, and Philippine origin are not, but output from Canadian material might duplicate a part of reported Canadian production.

There are indications that reserves of 170,000 ounces of palladium and 80,000 ounces of platinum could lie at Coronation Hill. Earlier political and environmental difficulties which threatened this development, have been removed as a result of government approval.

Helex Resources has been exploring the Fifield deposits—an area last worked at the turn of the century. A five-year drilling program to analyze the orebody is currently underway. Recent samples have suggested possible yields of 13.2 grams per tonne of platinum and 0.93 grams per tonne of palladium.

Hunter Resources has uncovered a South African Bushveld-type complex at Munni Munni in Western Australia. South Africa's General Mining group has explored chromite deposits in the Halls Creek region.

The United States Reserves

The Stillwater Mining Company in the USA is exploiting a 500-acre site some 80 miles southwest of Billings in southern Montana. The grade is estimated to be 13 to 22 grams per ton of platinum, with a platinum/palladium ratio of 1:3,5. Initial production began in March at a rate of 500 tonnes per day which will increase to 1,000 tonnes per day by 1992. Initial annual platinum output is expected to be 24,000 ounces rising eventually to 50,000 ounces. Palladium output is expected to rise from 75,000 ounces in 1987 to 150,000 ounces by 1992. Current reserves estimates suggest a 20- to 30-year project at Stillwater.

Russia

Platinum output in the Soviet Union is a product of nickel-copper mining, with nearly 90 percent of production from mines in the Norilsk region of northwestern

Platinum bars made in the USSR are very regular in their appearance. The circularly planed surface is characteristic. Apart from the hammer and sickle in the center and the mark Pt for platinum, the other marks represent the purity (bottom left), the weight in grams (bottom right) and the unique serial number of the bar (top left).

Siberia. A dearth of official information about current and planned production means that Soviet supply figures are only approximate and, therefore, may be suspect.

As revenue from energy exports increased with buoyant oil prices, during the 1970's and early 1980's, Soviet sales of platinum—an alternative hard currency earner—tended to decline. A reversal of the trend occurred in 1986 when Soviet platinum sales rose by 26 percent to 290,000 ounces. This compares with peak sales of 640,000 ounces in 1977. Soviet sales are expected to be maintained at 1986 levels in the 1990's, but a decline could not be ruled out because of increased internal consumption.

Other Minor Producers

China now produces sizeable amounts of nickel from nickel sulphide deposits at the city of Jinchang, in the Gansu Province of north central China. Like Soviet ore, China's reserves have a higher palladium than platinum content. Annual output of platinum group metals is not disclosed.

Minimal recoveries of platinum group metals have also been reported in refining operations conducted in Japan, Finland, Yugoslavia and the Philippines. Known deposits also exist in Zimbabwe, Ethiopia, Sierra Leone, the UK and in eastern Greenland. In South America, Columbia has long been a source, albeit in negligible amounts. Other possible significant projects are being examined in Brazil. As the platinum prices rachet upward, exploratory projects world-wide are likely to expand.

Table D

U.S. Imports for Consumption of Platinum-

Unwrought (troy ounces)

Year and Country	Platinum grains and nuggets	Sponge	Palladium	Iridium	Osmium
1984	19,786	1,527,841	1,795,939	18,225	1,630
1985	20,827	1,464,645	1,396,810	20,972	5,153
1986	10,465	1,713,971	1,387,131	30,368	5,776
1987	821	1,124,018	1,529,161	11,814	2,048
1988:					
Australia					
Belgium	1,035	47,394	162,630		
Canada	674	15,225	40,558		
Colombia	6,600	10,200			
Dom. Republic			22,964		
France		5,720			
Germany		42,628	33,087	2,381	
Hong Kong		1,964	34,720		
Israel					
Italy		7,625	10,652		
Ivory Coast			850		
Japan			9,192		
Mexico		79	50		
Netherlands		27,566	17,165	100	
Norway		10,001	855		
South Africa	1,700	916,454	656,442	14,512	1,600
Somalia			3,474		
Sweden					
Switzerland		2,098			
Taiwan	1,509		24,180		
U.S.S.R.	2,457	35,820	251,928		
U.K.	5,198	248,630	216,039	1,295	1,064
Other	172	300	2,954		
Total	**19,345**	**1,371,704**	**1,487,740**	**18,288**	**2,664**

Group Metals, by Year and Country

Osmiridium	Rhodium	Ruthenium	Unspecified combinations	Platinum-group metals from precious metal ores	Sweepings, waste, and scrap
150	155,671	198,257	8,822		526,738
	201,028	162,887	10,330	218	530,724
4,500	179,068	176,580	19,864	1,870	737,813
5,800	211,466	84,399	7,983	1,789	624,916
	673				4,934
	3,026				3,836
	247			135	168,706
				46	3,600
		9,857		161	5
	1,225				15
	1,531	351			4,356
	570				35,387
					2,084
	334				
		250			764
				297	74,451
	3,828	500	4		31
					4,610
	121,755	99,610			
					17,539
		50			1,928
					38,009
	38,035				
	59,007	9,763	15		46,399
	100		944		3,616
	230,331	**120,381**	**1,170**	**432**	**410,270**

Courtesy U.S. Bureau of Mines

4

Where Will We Get It in the Future?

There is a platinum shortage now, and it's getting worse for the reasons outlined in Chapter 2. The big question we face as we start the decade of the 1990's is—where will we get the platinum to make up the ever increasing gap?

The U.S. Bureau of Mines has studied this ongoing problem, concluding that alternative world sources to the Republic of South Africa for platinum and rhodium probably would not meet U.S. industrial demand. Non-South Africa world supply sources could be expected to meet only 40 percent of domestic platinum consumption and about 50 percent of rhodium requirements. However, there would be alternative world sources to South Africa for palladium and the other platinum group metals.

The Bureau of Mines followed up with another study that examined the impact on the gross national product (GNP) and the employment losses that would result from a U.S. embargo on South African platinum group metals. This study concluded that, assuming no change in the current emission control standards of the Clean Air Act, a decline in the level of automobile production and some substantial GNP losses were estimated to result from embargoing South African platinum and rhodium supplies. The estimated loss over a three-year period could be as high as U.S. $61 billion. The situation obviously is serious, and could become catastrophic due to retalitory effects of further economic sanctions against South Africa.

As a result of an embargo, dependence on Russia for platinum group metals would increase substantially. This dependency could increase by 30 percent almost immediately.

It is unknown, however, at this time whether Russia would sell us the additional needed supplies of these critical metals. Their need for additional hard currency would be an important consideration, but as previously pointed out, that could be offset by their ever expanding industrial requirements.

Increased Scrap Recovery and a Ban on Jewelry?

Recovering scrap from the electronics, petroleum refining and automobile catalytic converter is becoming an important and expanding source of platinum group metals helping to make up the shortfall that now exists.

In the electronics industry, such minute amounts

Automotive Catalysts: Rich Source of Precious Metals
Recovery levels (oz)*

Year	Platinum	Palladium	Rhodium
1984	94,010	35,370	1,390
1985	126,930	47,660	2,040
1986	160,080	60,370	2,930
1987	187,350	68,840	3,850
1988	210,190	76,610	5,770
1989	230,140	81,900	8,130
1990	248,120	88,490	11,760

*Estimated, based on trends in auto sales, PGM loadings, auto deregistration, scrap and salvage rates, and metal refinery recovery rates.

Source: Pt, Pd Review and Outlook 1984, J. Aron & Co.

are used in the various applications and their uses so widespread, that it makes recovery very difficult.

Therefore, as a source of supply in the future, it would be important, however small.

Cutting back on platinum being used in coinage, bars and jewelry could free up supplies for other more important uses as the shortage becomes more serious. The question is how would you mandate this? Hoarding would only increase. Ladies like their diamonds and platinum too much.

Price, however, would have its effect. U.S. $2,000 per ounce platinum could and temporarily probably would reduce the number of speculators and drastically reduce some uses.

The real hope, however, in the future will be finding substitutes to replace platinum group metals; not eliminating any of its uses.

In petroleum refining, its use is concentrated and in larger amounts making it easier to recover and reuse the platinum. Most of this platinum, however, never gets back into the supply chain to be used by other industries because the refiners reuse it themselves.

The case is different in the automobile catalytic converter after market. There are a predictable number of automobiles scrapped each year, and this keeps increasing as more cars are produced—thus a new industry has sprung up to recover this ever increasing amount of spent catalysts.

Perhaps a half million used catalytic converters are removed each month from scrapped autos, and are collected at centralized locations by scrap dealers, where they are sold to refiners. It has become an expanding and profitable business and is being looked to more and more as an important source of platinum group metals.

A higher price for platinum at some point could also cause some disinvestment of the metal on the part of the speculator or investor. This happened in the case of silver in the past. The problem here, however, is that there never has been much platinum bought and hoarded over the years like the other precious metals.

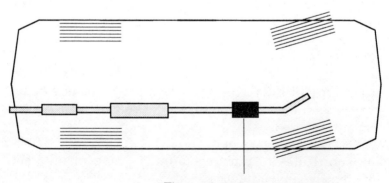

The autocatalyst is an integral part of the standard exhaust system

5

Geopolitics and Platinum

Political Upheaval in South Africa

With South Africa the primary source of platinum in the world today, attention is being focused on the possible effects of political events on this critical metal.

Whatever the political outcome in South Africa, it will have a significant influence on the future supply of platinum and its price structure. The shock and scope of this transition, of course, is incomprehensible at this time, because of the rapid changes taking place. At best, it looks ominous.

As this book is being written, the symbolic green,

gold and black flag of the African National Congress is being hoisted and unfurled over many areas of the Republic of South Africa. The ANC, formerly banned, has now been given legal status and can operate in the open as the recognized representative of the black majority. This organization remains dedicated to the takeover of the present government by demanding and exercising a yet-to-be-legalized constitutional change in the law mandating a one man one vote precept.

Pretoria has stopped short of this, envisioning instead a new constitution that balances and protects the interests of each race, where neither the whites or the blacks will dominate. This does not go far enough, and nothing less than a black-run government is acceptable to the ANC, the United States, and the United Nations.

In addition, they seek immediate abolition of the Population Registration Act, the Group Areas Act, the Land Acts and complete nationalization of the mines!

When and Why It Started

Few, if any, political writers, since Apartheid started after World War II, have ever questioned publicly why the government of the Republic of South Africa has been singled out for the vitriolic attacks it has sustained over the years from the United States and other western industrial nations.

Could it have to do with the fact that the land of South Africa is a geological freak of nature—a vast storehouse of mineral wealth, making it a target of those that need it and want it? Or is it just possible that South Africa's recalcitrance in not meekly going along with the major central banks in the de-emphasizing and demonetizing of gold have something to do with these attacks? If South Africa had not had these riches to flaunt, would anyone really care about the lack of political and economic power being withheld from the largely uneducated black majority? It is doubtful.

Maybe it is all happening because of the West's desperate need of these strategic minerals. Apartheid would have been made the holy cause, therefore, to mask the real objective—the control of the world's platinum and gold reserves.

The Present Situation

The present economic sanctions were put into effect in 1986 because previous pressures did not force the required change. The measure, passed over President Reagan's veto, banned imports of South African coal, textiles, uranium, agricultural products, iron and steel, oil, arms, computers and nuclear apparatus. Additionally, a suspension of U.S. loans and a prohibition of investment in the country was mandated—plus cancellation and stoppage of all air transport.

This economic pressure has only stiffened the resolve of the government, thereby resulting in the introduction of an even harsher sanctions bill than before by the U.S. Congress. (See Appendix A.) Because of all this, South Africa has become almost self sufficient and, except for an armed conflict resulting from an invasion, could probably survive for at least four more years.

Invasion Plans

Nothing short of total capitulation is being required of South Africa's present government. If sanctions don't do the job, then a gold boycott, a naval blockade, or a stopping of all trade from other countries will be imposed, and in the event these measures don't work, then the grand plan calls for armed conflict—an invasion, if you will! And military occupation!

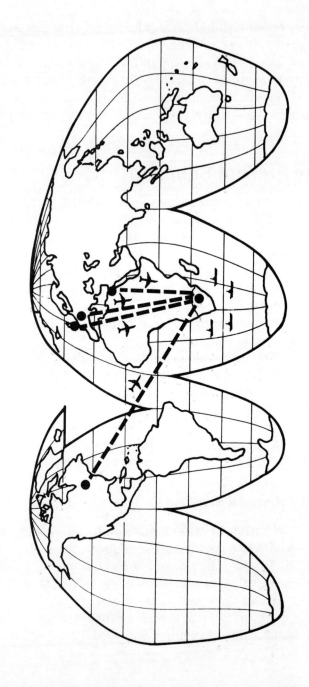

Departure Points and Routes That Could Be Used for Invasion of South Africa

Detailed plans for an invasion and occupation of South Africa have been drawn up and are in place at this time. This rather benign sounding tome, a 170-page document, titled *Apartheid and United Nations Collective Measures*—an analysis by A.C. Leiss, prepared under the auspices of The Carnegie Endowment for International Peace, lays out in finite detail a blockade and invasion plan of South Africa by United Nations Forces; that body being the designated instrumentality to carry it out. It reads like a book by Tom Clancy. Experiencd experts in every specialty were drawn on for input including that from the U.S. military forces in preparing this document.

Exact numbers of troops, aircraft, carriers, supply troop ships, landing craft and airborne brigades are documented. Timetables as to how long it would take to subdue South African forces and the estimated number of casualties the United Nations Force would suffer are specifically spelled out. A dollar cost breakdown is included covering men and equipment, leaving little to the imagination. The morbidly curious could quite easily, with a hand calculator, figure out the cost allocated to kill each South African defender, should they so wish.

What is more shocking to me about this document is that such an alternative as an invasion and military occupation was or still is being seriously considered at all—especially by an organization presumably so dedicated to world peace. Historians in the future decades from now will make a final judgment.

So whether the black majority violently dispenses with the present government and white minority rule; or it is eliminated by a U.N. sponsored invasion, seems really immaterial. Peace will be achieved finally—but in all likelihood posthumously for the white minority.

The Carnegie Endowment for International Peace

The Carnegie Endowment for International Peace, headquartered in Washington D.C., was founded in 1910 by Andrew Carnegie. An operating foundation, it conducts its own programs of research, discussion, publication and education in international relations and U.S. foreign policy.

The staff of 62 consists of Senior Associates, Resident Associates and their assistants who bring to their work extensive first-hand experience in foreign affairs. Their background includes government, journalism and public affairs, including significant overseas service.

Their projects, past and present, cover a broad range of policy issues—military, political and economic. Through writing, public and media appearances, etc., their staff attempts to influence and direct foreign policy of the U.S. and that of the United Nations.

Because of this close association with government, where their staff members have served in key slots like that of the U.S. Senate Armed Services Committee, one would have to conclude that much of major foreign policy enacted in the U.S. is formulated and set by this group.

Former Endowment professionals read like a *Who's Who* of government, industry and banking, over the years. Well-known names like Robert McNamara, Paul Warnke, James Baker, C. Fred Bergsten and McGeorge Bundy are among the many alumni of this organization. The Carnegie Endowment is considered to be an arm of *the invisible government* and frequently influences foreign policy. (See Appendix B.)

Platinum After the Takeover

The platinum and gold mines of South Africa are expected to be nationalized after the takeover by the ANC. Prior to this, however, there could be serious sabotage causing an interruption of platinum group metal production. Any interruption in platinum availability, regardless of the time span, would have an immediate and significant effect on the price of the metal.

Production at these mines would also tail off, in all probability, due to the temporary lack of white technical supervisors to operate them, again increasing the shortage of platinum.

AIDS Effect on Platinum

Another problem, perhaps even more serious, is the spread of AIDS. Workers for the platinum mines in South Africa are brought in from the neighboring countries for a specified period of time and then returned to their homes and families. The South African Chamber of Mines monitors the health of these workers and treats them for any illness. Because of this AIDS epidemic sweeping black Africa, the Chamber of Mines is screening all these workers on an ongoing basis in an attempt to control the spread of this deadly disease. AIDS has already paralyzed Zambia's copper mining industry, with over half of its qualified workers already dead, and it is estimated that the number of individuals infected with AIDS in Black Africa is doubling each year. The quality of health care now being given these workers is expected to decrease when the ANC takes over. Mining output can be expected to be directly affected, further decreasing the supply, thus adding to the upward pressure on the price of platinum.

6

Expected Price Explosion

U.S. $2,300 per ounce platinum? The U.S. Bureau of Mines says it will happen (chart p. 59). A special study titled "Estimated Direct Economic Impact of a U.S. Import Embargo On Strategic and Critical Minerals Produced In South Africa" not only details and projects this price level of platinum but says it will happen quickly (Appendix D).

The following are the " Major Assumptions Underlying the Analysis by the U.S. Bureau of Mines of the Impact of a United States Embargo on South African Platinum Imports."

• No South African production is supplied to the United States.

• As a result of the U.S. unilateral embargo, two markets are created:

1. A United States demand and non-South African supply market.

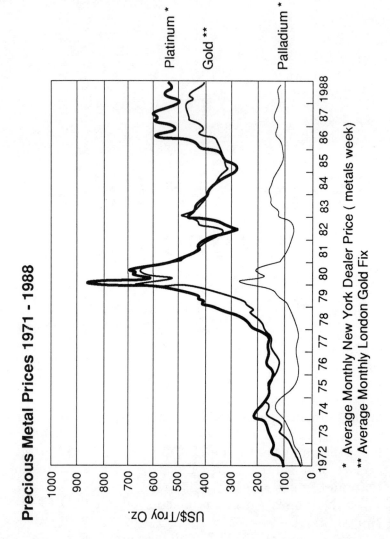

Precious Metal Prices 1971 - 1988

US$/Troy Oz.

Platinum *

Gold **

Palladium *

* Average Monthly New York Dealer Price (metals week)
** Average Monthly London Gold Fix

2. A rest-of-Western world demand and supply market.

• Western market trade pattern adjustments may occur immediately, under which all non-South African Western world market supplies are made available to the United States.

• As a result of the persistent, high platinum prices during the impact period (four years):

1. Domestic recycling of platinum from auto catalysts increases to the estimated recovery potential in the study period:

a. The baseline provides for recycling to increase from 75 thousand ounces to 327 thousand ounces.

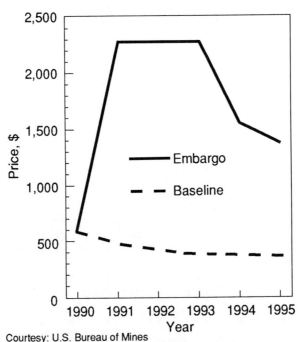

Embargo Impacts: U.S. Platinum Price (1990 dollars per troy ounce)

Courtesy: U.S. Bureau of Mines

b. In the embargo scenario, recycling reaches 300 thousand ounces in 1989 and 1990. In 1991 and 1992 recycling is increased to 550 thousand ounces.

2. Domestic primary production expands, from a base of 25,000 ounces in the first year of the embargo to:

a. 50,000 ounces in the second year (of the embargo).

b. 100,000 ounces in the third year and thereafter.

3. Primary (rather than byproduct) production capacity in Canada and Australia is brought on-line. In the third year of the embargo, production capacity (and United States supply) increases by 250,000 ounces and is main-

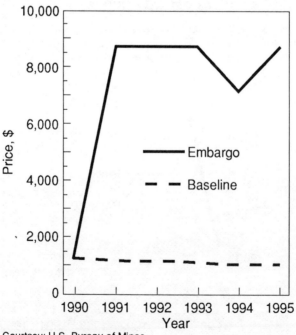

Embargo Impacts: U.S. Rhodium Price (1990 dollars per troy ounce)

Courtesy: U.S. Bureau of Mines

tained at that level in the fourth and fifth years of the embargo.

4. Soviet Bloc sales to the West are maintained at a normal level, although all of these sales are exported to the United States during the embargo.

If their projections are to be believed, then it should be pointed out that rhodium, a platinum group metal which is even more important than platinum, has already seen a price move from U.S. $1,200 per ounce to over U.S. $2,100 per ounce!

Rhodium, says the before mentioned report, will go to over U.S. $8,000 per ounce! (See chart page 60.)

Their maximum projected price levels for the platinum group metals have been worked out by experts using current and carefully collated data. The expected price explosion, when it happens, would leave little time for the investor to react. From past history and experience, major capital gains opportunities are often missed because even the most informed investors frequently think that they have adequate time to buy before a large price move. Often this procrastination causes them to miss the boat altogether.

We are also seeing today a platinum price pattern that is becoming more and more independent of that of gold because industrial demand for gold is insignificant compared to platinum. This is causing platinum to be considered even more precious by precious metal investors and the price gap of over U.S. $100 is widening.

Inflation Effect

Independent of the many other variables affecting platinum's price, inflation's impact will probably become even more visible and significant in the 1990's.

Normal inflation over the past decade in the five percent range has now suddenly rocketed upward into

double-digit levels and higher. Hyperinflation has ar-
rived, and all signs indicate that the situation is out of
control.

Because of this, a renewed flight from the dollar has
started and will continue to escalate due to the trillion
dollar Federal and Third World debt, the massive financial failures and the staggering balance of payments
problem. The gargantuan monetary and economic issues
facing the U.S. plus the insatiable needs of the emerging
East-bloc countries spells disaster for stable prices.

We are caught in a savage inflationary spiral that
could take the prices of goods and services up by more than
30 percent. Investors seeking protection of any form, as
they have in all previous calamitous times, will bid up the
price of platinum even more than the price of gold, making
the projection of $2,300 per ounce seem like a bargain.

7

How Platinum Could Make You Rich

Platinum could make you rich if you were to buy into any one or more of the investments connected with this metal prior to their price moving up appreciably. Such a price move, of course, is not guaranteed, and it may or may not occur and/or if it does occur, it could do so in a time frame outside of the period of your entrance into the market causing you to be in a loss position. Under the circumstances, the investments mentioned here may not be suitable for certain accounts, and it is advisable that you consult your broker or advisor prior to making any decision to invest.

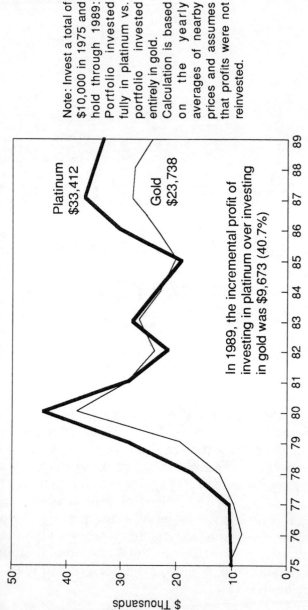

Platinum Yields Higher Long-term Profits Than Investing in Gold

Platinum Yielded a 40.7% Higher Profit Than Gold Over The Past 15 Years

Platinum
$33,412

Gold
$23,738

In 1989, the incremental profit of investing in platinum over investing in gold was $9,673 (40.7%)

Note: Invest a total of $10,000 in 1975 and hold through 1989: Portfolio invested fully in platinum vs. portfolio invested entirely in gold. Calculation is based on the yearly averages of nearby prices and assumes that profits were not reinvested.

$ Thousands

Platinum Bars

Platinum can be purchased in the form of one- and 10-ounce bars in large quantities from refiners such as Johnson Matthey or Englehardt Minerals. Smaller amounts can be obtained from any one of a number of coin dealers in the U.S. or overseas. One of the most respected is, of course, Blanchard and Company in New Orleans. (See Recommended Sources .)

Platinum in bar form is considered perhaps the least expensive way to buy, that way you are not paying a seigniorage charge added on to the price of the metal. The process of making platinum bars obviously is a lot less complicated and inexpensive than making coins.

Kilo bars and larger size platinum bars are more popular in Japan and other areas of the world and can be obtained there. Be aware that there could be a danger of counterfeit bars in any size if platinum continues to increase in price. Any purchase made should only be done with and through bona fide firms.

Platinum bars

Platinum Coins

Platinum coins have proved to be a very popular form of investment in the past and are definitely on the increase today because more new "big country" coins are being offered for sale.

Russia issued the first platinum coins back about 1825 through 1845 in one-, three-, and six-ruble denomination. These were very small issues and since have become collectors' items. A six-ruble coin recently sold for U.S. $24,000 in New York. Experts think these coins eventually like Fabergé Eggs will become priceless.

Most platinum coins being issued today are legal tender coins; meaning they are actual coins of the issuing country.

Other coins are investment type coins or commemorative coins issued by private mints or refiners. Popular coins in this category are the Platinum Dragon, a one-ounce coin, an issue of Johnson Matthey and a big seller in the Orient. Another is the Prospector, also one ounce, issued by Englehardt—a steady seller in the U.S.

Legal tender coins made of platinum are now being offered by the Isle of Man, Canada and Australia. Russia may issue one soon also.

The Isle of Man, Platinum Noble, is issued in one-ounce and smaller sizes and can be obtained through any reputable coin dealer. This coin has proven to be very popular, not only as an investment item, but is used in jewelry as well.

The Canadian Platinum Maple Leaf is an exact replica of the previously issued gold and silver Maple Leaf, which proved to be so popular with investors. The only difference in this one-ounce coin and those, is that it is made pure of pure platinum and so indicated on the coin and, of course, the price is over U.S. $100 higher than the gold Maple Leaf. These coins can be purchased through any branch of any of the main banks of Canada and/or your coin dealer. The Canadian Platinum Maple Leaf seems to have captured the number one spot with investors, pushing aside for the moment the Isle of Man Noble.

The platinum Maple Leaf launched by the Royal Canadian Mint in November 1988 complements the gold Maple Leaf, which has been in circulation for several years. Like the Koala, the platinum Maple Leaf is issued in 1 oz, 1/2 oz, 1/4 oz, and 1/10 oz sizes.

Australia's Platinum Koala one-ounce coin has come on the investment scene only recently and hasn't become completely established yet. As it gains acceptance with investors, more dealers will stock it.

It might be noted here that platinum coins generally sell for more than the spot price of the metal than does the bars. Coins are minted in limited numbers each year

and, therefore, can appreciate more as each issue becomes more scarce. If you choose coins as an investment, keep in mind that you are not only betting on an increase in the price of platinum but also on the future numismatic value of the particular coin. Be aware that there is a danger of counterfeit coins, and this danger will increase with the rise in the price of platinum.

Platinum Stocks

Platinum stocks, or shares, generally can be broken down into the South African primary producers and the Canadian exploration companies which would also include companies that are involved in platinum secondary recovery from scrapped catalytic converters.

The primary producers—the South African stocks, such as Rustenburg Platinum and Impala Platinum are listed in the South African and London stock exchanges, and the ordinary shares can be purchased through any brokerage firm in either place. In the U.S., investors can buy American Depository Receipt shares only. These are generally known as ADR's and can be purchased through most brokerage firms at this writing. The situation could change, however, regarding the South Africa platinum stocks because of the sanctions bill now before the U.S. Congress, which specifically prohibits ownership and/or purchase by U.S. citizens of these stocks.

At the present time, it is estimated that 25 percent of these shares are now held by U.S. accounts. If this legislation is passed, these accounts would be forced to dispose of these shares or face a substantial penalty. This obviously could have a depressing effect on the price of South Africa platinum shares.

That would be the time to buy them. Nathan Rothschild so advised in 1815 when he said, "The time to buy is when blood is running in the street." History may repeat itself in regards to the South African platinum stocks.

The Canadian Platinum Stocks

There are a handful of Canadian platinum stocks that may be affected by a substantial price move in platinum. Typically investors will be looking at any and all investments that have any connection with platinum— real or imagined.

Stocks such as Madeleine Mines and American Platinum and Overseas Platinum are three such companies, that are small, speculative issues listed on the Vancouver and the Toronto Stock Exchanges that are involved in exploration for platinum group metals in Canada, the United States and Brazil. These stocks have been substantially higher in past markets and could get very active again if platinum prices were to go into orbit. Presently these issues would be categorized as penny stocks. Cheap stocks such as these often are sought after by speculators when metals prices and inflation run rampant.

Another Canadian stock to be watched, also listed on the Vancouver Stock Exchange will be U.S. Platinum because this company is involved with the recovery of platinum from scrapped automobile catalytic converters. This issue, also a speculative stock, has been up to $6 per share in the past. Companies involved in platinum scrap recovery like U.S. Platinum could be singled out if we have an embargo on platinum exports from South Africa because of economic sanctions effected by the U.S. By the way, about 29 ounces of platinum is recovered from every tonne of auto-catalyst material as compared to about one-quarter ounce from platinum mine concentrates.

Again Canada platinum stocks can be bought through any U.S. or Canadian brokerage firm and would

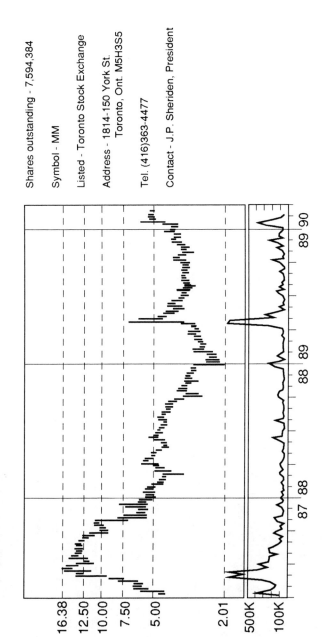

Madeleine Mines Ltd

Shares outstanding - 7,594,384

Symbol - MM

Listed - Toronto Stock Exchange

Address - 1814-150 York St.
          Toronto, Ont. M5H3S5

Tel. (416)363-4477

Contact - J.P. Sheriden, President

U.S. Platinum, Inc.

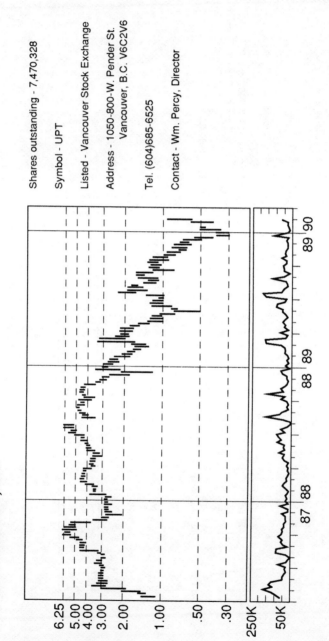

Shares outstanding - 7,470,328

Symbol - UPT

Listed - Vancouver Stock Exchange

Address - 1050-800-W. Pender St.
         Vancouver, B.C. V6C2V6

Tel. (604)685-6525

Contact - Wm. Percy, Director

Overseas Platinum Corp.

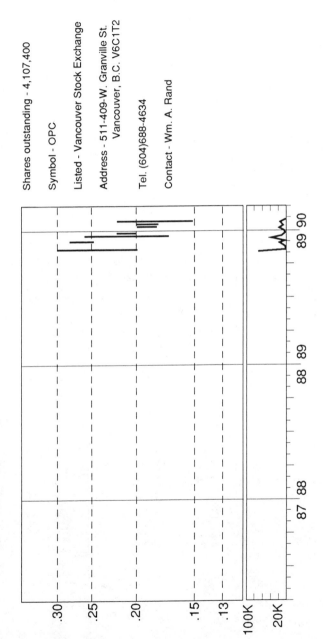

Shares outstanding - 4,107,400

Symbol - OPC

Listed - Vancouver Stock Exchange

Address - 511-409-W. Granville St.
Vancouver, B.C. V6C1T2

Tel. (604)688-4634

Contact - Wm. A. Rand

American Platinum Inc.

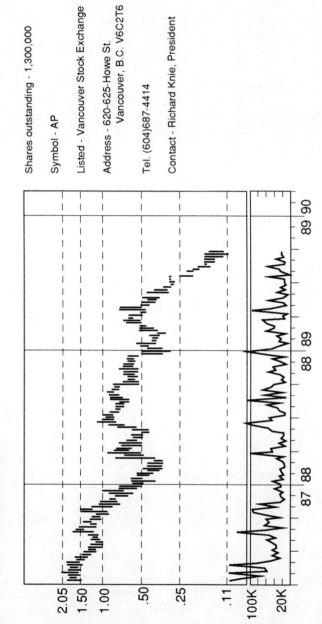

Shares outstanding - 1,300,000

Symbol - AP

Listed - Vancouver Stock Exchange

Address - 620-625-Howe St.
          Vancouver, B.C. V6C2T6

Tel. (604)687-4414

Contact - Richard Knie, President

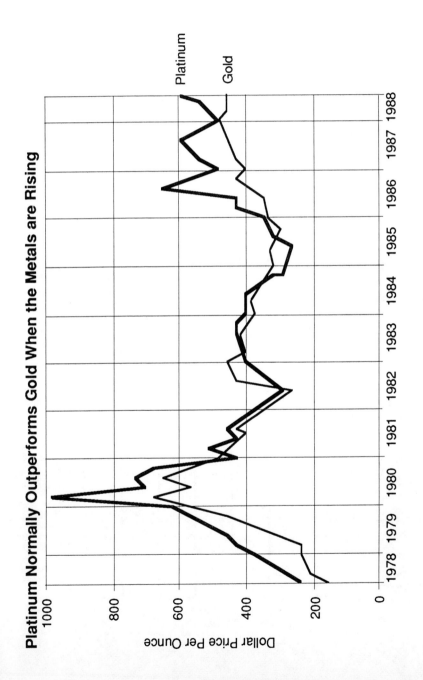

Platinum Normally Outperforms Gold When the Metals are Rising

5 Year Price Performance
December 31, 1984 - December 31, 1989

% Change

Platinum + 75.5%

Gold + 39.6%

Long Term Bonds + 8%

Trade Weighted Dollar
(Morgan Guaranty) -31.8%

Source: Data Resources Inc.

not be subject to restriction by the passage of additional economic sanctions by the U.S.

Platinum Futures

Future trading in platinum is another investment avenue open to investors at this time who think that the price of platinum will appreciate.

This route can be even more risky than that of the so-called penny stocks. Anyone thinking of speculating in platinum futures should certainly consult with an expert first at one of the many good commodity firms.

Platinum future contracts, as with most commodities, can give the investor control over a substantial amount of metal over a given period of time for a fraction of its actual value. If the price goes up, an enormous amount of money can be made depending, of course, on the number of contracts held. The reverse, of course, can be utter disaster.

Platinum or any other commodity futures are ultra speculative and certainly are not for the faint hearted. Remember, nothing goes straight up including platinum, and if it does, it will have done it in a series of jagged moves, any one of which could wipe you out if you were on the wrong side of the market. Keep in mind even if the price of platinum were to go to U.S. $2,300 per ounce, a lot of people could suffer a loss because of the ensuing volatility.

Trading in platinum futures is done in the U.S. through the New York Mercantile Exchange and in Tokyo on the Tokyo Commodity Exchange. Japan now leads the U.S. in trading volume in platinum, and it was just reported that the combined volume from these two exchanges already amounts to over 38 times annual world production.

8

A Second Opinion—How Others See It

Opportunity rarely presents itself in a manner that can be viewed clearly and simply as black or white. It is a judgment call at best.

My analysis and conclusion as to the direction that the price of platinum will take, may seem totally valid and unflawed in my mind, but in the minds of others, the difference of opinion could be skewed by as much as 180 degrees.

Disparity in viewpoint and variance in conclusions tend to be the norm rather than the exception in the stock and commodity markets. If this were not so and it was that easy, obviously everybody would be rich.

The important thought to be considered here, however, so that you can clarify your own thinking, is where are these other people coming from? Do they have an ax to grind, so to speak? Are they wishful thinkers? Is their head in the sand? Do they stand to gain by their attempt or effort to affect the market? Or are they just uninformed? And finally, and even more importantly, is their view or are their concerns backed up by facts *at the time*, keeping in mind the frequency at which things can change?

For example, what was really in the mind of the Chairman of Ford Motor Company and what was his intent when he made the statement that a substitute was found for platinum in automobile catalytic converters? Was Ford Motor Company having a problem getting platinum and at the right price? His statement affected the market dramatically at the time. Later study of his statement by experts and research people indicated that this was not true—that there was no alternative to platinum for use in catalytic converters—and so the price went back up.

As pointed out in Chapter 2, in the commodity market where platinum futures are traded daily, rumors run rampant. Each and every rumor at the time more or less affects the price. Traders or others that create these stories do so to benefit themselves even though such activity is totally illegal, but it continues because it is often impossible to prove. Commodity traders want markets to be volatile, otherwise they wouldn't make money. It is therefore difficult sometimes to get a true opinion based on facts from people in the commodity business. They either don't know or don't want to know, especially the long-term picture.

Users of platinum will also have a different opinion than producers or mining companies. Refiners' opinions will be different than those of users and mining companies. They (the refiners) would tend to keep a neutral viewpoint or stance on the price of platinum in order to keep both sides happy.

Stock and bond market analysts and brokers generally have little or no knowledge of the precious metal's markets and in the case of platinum, they would know almost nothing. If you even asked for an opinion about the direction of the price of platinum, in all likelihood, you would get a jumbled confused answer or a negative reply. If precious metals prices are going up, that means overall stock and bond market prices would likely be going down—and that would be something most brokers don't want to admit to. Their bread and butter comes from up markets for stocks.

Even the U.S. government statisticians that compute the consumer price index and the politicians that have to live with those figures have a built-in bias regarding precious metals' prices.

If the consumer price index is moving up significantly, it is an admission that inflation is worsening. The public, viewing those figures, perceives and often concludes the same thing and react by attempting to hedge against this rising inflation by buying precious metals.

That is exactly what our government doesn't want us to do because this in effect means there is an increase in the flight from the dollar. It is their intent to keep precious metals' prices from rising, so that they won't reflect the accelerating inflation. Inflation is the biggest domestic threat that a party in power and the accompanying bureaucratic apparatus has to face. History has proven that they will say or do anything necessary to stop or contain inflation because it is so politically damaging, and that means if it becomes necessary, even manipulating precious metals' prices.

Fortunately for the investing public, the media and communication network is so vast and efficient that it makes it much more difficult for those who would attempt to "doctor" the news, to be successful in this effort.

So getting back to platinum and the projected price rise, one can guess that there are many groups and companies, including the U.S. Government, that would be adversely affected if the price were to rise.

It can be concluded, therefore, that these groups would do almost anything to keep it from happening including the most latent deception or even war!

9

Platinum—The Pluses And Minuses

In making any investment decision, it is vitally important to apprise yourself of all the information available at the time in order to come up with the right answer. If your decision is based on misinformation and/or there are gaps in the information that is available, then it makes obviously much more difficult to make a sound assessment of the situation.

The platinum predicament is one of these situations. So here is a summary of the pluses and minuses as I see them.

Why Platinum's Price Will Go Up

1. An already existing shortfall is widening.

2. Increased uses for platinum are being found in industry and in the field of medicine.

3. Catalytic converter markets are getting bigger due to more automobiles being manufactured.

4. Former Iron Curtain country markets are opening up.

5. Worldwide inflation is taking place.

5. Jewelry markets are expanding.

7. Sanctions are increasing against South Africa.

8. Catalytic converters are becoming more necessary in many cities and may become mandatory even for motor bikes.

9. Increased hoarding or investment in platinum is taking place due to a falling U.S. dollar, third world debt and a persistent trade deficit.

10. Coinage is increasing by more countries.

11. Armed conflict is possible with South Africa.

12. Possibility of platinum being used in cold fusion would open up a vast new market for platinum.

Why Platinum's Price May Not Go Up

Many of the reasons mentioned here may be highly improbable.

1. Substitutes may be found.

2. Controls could or may be put on the price of platinum.

3. Trading may be suspended and/or holding of platinum could be prohibited.

4. Inflation may subside.

5. Mandatory use of catalytic converters may change.

6. Sanctions against South Africa may be cancelled or lifted.

7. There won't be any more uses discovered for platinum.

8. Former communist countries will decide not to mandate catalytic converters.

9. Countries producing platinum coins will discontinue this practice.

10. Major new reserves of platinum group metals may be found in the U.S. and Canada.

11. More platinum will be recovered from scrap and auto catalysts than before.

So, you can see by now there are numerous reasons, facts, guesses, estimates and judgments that could and will affect platinum. In making a decision to profit from the price rise that I project, you will have to weigh carefully all of the information available as I have done. In doing so, you may not reach the same conclusion. Whatever you do, keep in mind that there are no guarantees.

10

Platinum's Future—Fusion?

The scientific community in the U.S. was stunned on March 23, 1989, when it was announced at a specifically called public press conference that two University of Utah professors, Stanley Pons and Martin Fleischmann had sustained fusion in a test jar at room temperature in the school laboratory. The uproar and outcry in reaction to this announcement that followed in the media by fellow scientists was almost unparalleled in its ferocity and savageness.

They were accused of committing numerous improprieties running from deception to unprofessionalism; in spite of the fact, the experiment, if proven and developed, could change the world by solving mankind's energy problems forever by providing a source of virtually limitless power. This process would generate no pollutants and would give off even less radiation than nuclear power plants.

B. Stanley Pons and Martin Fleischmann filled a bottle with heavy water (which consists of oxygen and an isotope of hydrogen called deuterium) mixed in lithium salts. In it they immersed a palladium electrode wrapped with a coil of platinum. After running current through it for about two weeks, they said, the palladium began to heat up - releasing four times the amount of heat as the energy they put in.

Cold Fusion Experiment

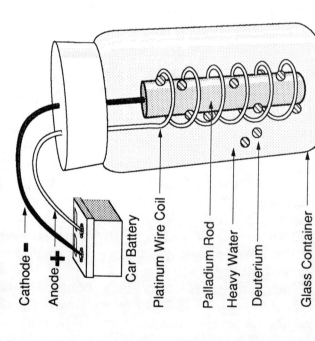

Cathode ■
Anode ✚

Car Battery

Platinum Wire Coil

Palladium Rod

Heavy Water

Deuterium

Glass Container

So why all the paranoia and jealousy over cold fusion on the part of the scientific establishment? Could it have to do with fusion research grants being given by the Federal Government and—maybe who would be receiving all the laurels and glory? Billions have already been spent on hot fusion experiments since the first man-made fusion was produced by H-bomb explosions in the 1950's and billions more could be spent but could be diverted to cold fusion development instead. The present scientific establishment, eating at the government trough, has demonstrated that they will fight to the death to prevent this from happening.

In spite of all the vitriolic counter claims regarding the viability and reality of cold fusion, two Japanese research teams recently have turned up solid evidence verifying the original experiments of Pons and Fleischmann. Both Japanese teams perceived what was considered sustained amounts of neutron radiation, an obvious sign that fusion has occurred. The very presence of neutron emissions in this type of experiment is a signal of success. Other teams in the U.S. and in other countries continue their experimentation in this field. The payoff could be limitless for those who succeed.

Success with cold fusion could mean the elimination of many other sources of energy and power, thereby, vaulting platinum group metals into a prominent position.

This would send the price of platinum up to an unimaginable level while at the same time eliminating it in its use in many present day industrial applications.

Whatever additional events or discoveries that take place effecting platinum's future, the net result will be less platinum available and at a much higher price, rewarding those investors that were perceptive enough to have bought it early.

EPILOGUE

This book, although about platinum, may seem to the reader to get a little far afield and into other areas that might not have a direct relationship to the subject. This was not my intention when I started to write this book, but my research took me down many indirect and crooked paths in order to find and confirm certain bits of information that had a direct bearing on platinum and/or its price pattern. In this endeavor, hopefully, I have left nothing out.

The conclusions reached here are my own and no guarantees are implied or expressed as to the future price of platinum. The reader is on his own. What may seem to be a certainty can often turn out to be just the opposite. Logical consequences of specific economic events can be altered or markedly influenced by political or military actions upon the part of governments or others.

There is no "inside" information in this book. Everything discussed, including the report by The Carnegie Endowment For Peace, is public information. I must admit, however, that some public information is more difficult to get than others.

As this book goes to press, certain events affecting the price of platinum are unfolding quite rapidly. Hopefully, you will have had the opportunity to react to it before too much time has passed and the price of platinum has gotten away.

James E. Ryan

Appendix A

House of Representatives Sanctions Legislation now before the U.S. Congress. The Senate bill is identical.

101st Congress
1st Session

H.R. 21

To prohibit investments in, and certain other activities with respect to, South Africa, and for other purposes.

IN THE HOUSE OF REPRESENTATIVES
JANUARY 3, 1989

Mr. Dellums (for himself, Mr. Ackerman, Mr. Akaka, Mr. Bennett, Mr. Berman, Mrs. Boxer, Mr. Clay, Mr. Coyne, Mr. Crockett, Mr. DeFazio, Mr. Donnelly, Mr. Downey, Mr. Dymally, Mr. Evans, Mr. Fauntroy, Mr. Florio, Mr. Frank, Mr. Hoyer, Mr. Kastenmeier, Mr. Kennedy, Mr. Kleczka, Mr. Jacobs, Mr. Levin of Michigan, Mr. Levine of California, Mr. Lewis of Georgia, Mr. Markey, Mr. Mavroules, Mr. Mfume, Mr. Mineta, Mr. Moody, Ms.

Pelosi, Ms. Oakar, Mr. Roybal, Mr. Sabo, Mr. Shays, Mr. Stark, Mr. Torres, Mr. Udall, Mr. Vento, Mr. Weiss, Mr. Wheat, Mr. Wise, and Mr. Wyden) introduced the following bill; which was referred jointly to the Committees on Foreign Affairs, Armed Services, Banking, Finance and Urban Affairs, Energy and Commerce, Permanent Select Committee on Intelligence, Interior and Insular Affairs, Ways and Means, and Rules

May 8, 1989

Additional sponsors: Mr. Bryant, Mr. Cardin, Mr. Sikorski, Mrs. Morella, Mr. Foglietta, Mr. Ford of Tennessee, Mr. Fascell, Mr. Waxman, Mr. Smith of Florida, Mr. Gephardt, Mr. Brennan, Mr. Bates, Mr. Atkins, Mr. Gray, Mrs. Collins, Mr. Edwards of California, Mr. Panetta, Mr. Stokes, Mr. Dixon, Mr. Hawkins, Mr. Hayes of Illinois, Mr. Glickman, Mr. Hochbrueckner, Mr. Gibbons, Mr. Hughes, Mr, Eckart, Mr. Costello, Mr. Bilbray, Mr. Morrison of Connecticut, Mr. Moakley, Mr. Gejdenson, Mr. Owens of New York, Mr. Lehman of California, Mr. Savage, Mr. Rose, Mr. Traficant, Mr. Conyers, Mr. Miller of California, Mr. Flake, Mr. Traxler, Mr. Perkins, Mr. Towns, Mr. Leland, Mr. AuCoin, Mrs. Schroeder, Mr. Payne of New Jersey, Mr. Pease, Mr. Rangel, Mr. Nagle, Mr. Feighan, Mr. Espy, Mr. Williams, Mr. Brown of California, Mr. Leach of Iowa, Ms. Kaptur, Mr. Synar, Mr. Bustamante, Mr. de Lugo, Mr. Durbin, Mr. Fazio, Mr. Gilman, Mr. Gonzalez, Mr. Kildee, Mr. Jontz, Mr. Lehman of Florida, Mrs. Lowey of New York, Mr. Thomas A. Luken, Mr. McDermott, Mr. Pickett, Mr. Richardson, Mr. Robinson, Ms. Schneider, Mr. Scheuer, Mr. Solarz, Mr. Murphy, Mr. Campbell of Colorado, Mr. Rahall, Mr. Hertel, Mr. Pepper, Mr. Oberstar, Mr. Lantos, Mr. Garcia, and Mr. Conte

A BILL

To prohibit investments in, and certain other activities with respect to, South Africa, and for other purposes.

Be it enacted by the Senate and House of Representatives of the United States of America in Congress assembled,

SECTION 1. SHORT TITLE; REFERENCES; TABLE OF CONTENTS.

(a) Short Title—This Act may be cited as the "Anti-Apartheid Act Amendments of 1989."

(b) References—References in this Act to "the Act" are the Comprehensive Anti-Apartheid Act of 1986.

(c) Table of Contents—

TITLE II—SANCTIONS AGAINST SOUTH AFRICAN IMPORTS INTO THE UNITED STATES

TITLE III—GENERAL PROVISIONS

Sec. 301. Technical and Conforming Amendments.
Sec. 302. Effective date.

TITLE I—SANCTIONS AGAINST INVESTMENT IN,
AND EXPORTS TO, SOUTH AFRICA AND OTHER
MEASURES (EXCEPT IMPORT RESTRICTIONS)
TO END APARTHEID

Part A—Amendments to the Comprehensive Anti-
Apartheid Act of 1986 and Other Laws

Sec. 101. Prohibitions on investment in South Africa.

(a) Prohibitions on Investment—Effective 180 days after the date of the enactment of this Act, section 301 of the Comprehensive Anti-Apartheid Act of 1986 (hereafter in this Act referred to as "the Act") is amended to read as follows:

"Prohibition on Investment in South Africa

"Sec. 301. (a) Subject to subsections (b) and (c), a United States person may not purchase, acquire, own, or hold any investment in South Africa.

"(b) The prohibition under subsection (a) shall not apply to any investment in a business enterprise owned and controlled by South Africans economically and politically disadvantaged by apartheid where such business enterprise is and continues to be not less than 90 percent owned by, and under the control of, South Africans economically and politically disadvantaged by apartheid.

"(c)(1) Notwithstanding subsection (a), any individual described in paragraph (2), may continue to own and hold investments in South Africa during any period and to the extent that such investments are considered South African emigrant non-resident assets and subject to restrictions on their transfer or disposition under the exchange control regulations of the Government of South

Africa (promulgated pursuant to the Currency and Exchange Act of 1933 and as in effect on June 2, 1988) which limit the ability of such an individual to comply with the prohibitions under subsection (a).

"(2) An individual, for purposes of paragraph (1), is an individual who, on the date of the enactment of the Anti-Apartheid Act Amendments of 1989, is—

"(A) a former citizen or resident of South Africa; and

"(B)(i) a citizen of the United States; or

"(ii) an alien lawfully admitted for permanent residence in the United States."

(b) Waiver—A person affected by the prohibition under section 301 of the Comprehensive Anti-Apartheid Act of 986 (as amended by subsection (a)) may apply to the President for a one-time waiver of the prohibition. With respect to any applicant, the President may waive the application of section 301 for not more than 180 days after such section takes effect. Such waiver may be granted only for good cause. During any period of waiver under this subsection, the provisions of the Comprehensive Anti-Apartheid Act of l986 as in effect before the date of the enactment of the Anti-Apartheid Act Amendments of 1989 shall apply and the President may not waive any such provision.

(c) Negotiations With Employee Organizations Regarding Termination of Investment—(a) A controlled South African entity, subject to the investment prohibition under section 301 of the Comprehensive Anti-Apartheid Act of l986 (as amended by subsection (a)), that employs more than 24 South Africans economically and politically disadvantaged by apartheid—

(A) shall notify all such South African employees and their employee organizations of a termination of investment not less than 90 days prior to such termination; and

(B) shall enter into good faith negotiations with trade unions representing such disadvantaged South Africans (or with other representative worker organizations if there are no such unions) regarding the terms of a termination.

(2) Negotiations under paragraph (1)(B) shall include discussions and agreements concerning pension benefits; relocation of employees; continuation of existing union recognition agreements; severance pay; and acquisition of the terminated business or the business assets by entities representing South Africans economically and politically disadvantaged by apartheid including trade unions, union-sponsored workers' trusts, other representative worker organizations, and employees.

Sec. 102. Prohibition on Exports to South Africa.

Effective 180 days after the date of the enactment of this Act, section 303 of the Act is amended to read as follows:

"PROHIBITION OF EXPORTS TO SOUTH AFRICA FROM THE UNITED STATES

"Sec. 303. (a) No goods or technology subject to the jurisdiction of the Untied States may be exported, or re-exported, to South Africa. No goods or technology may be exported, or re-exported, to South Africa by any person subject to the jurisdiction of the United States.

"(b) The prohibitions under subsection (a) shall not apply to—

"(1) publications, including books, newspapers, magazines, films, television programming, phonograph records, video and audio tape recordings, photographs, microfilm, microfiche, posters, and similar materials;

"(2) donations of articles intended to relieve human suffering, such as food, clothing, and medicine and medical supplies intended strictly for medical purposes;

"(3) commercial sales of agricultural commodities and products; and

"(4) goods and technology for use in the gathering or

dissemination of information by news media organizations subject to the jurisdiction of the Untied States which
provide an assurance to the Secretary of State that such
goods and technology will not be used, leased, sold, or
transferred to any South African entity.

"(c) The prohibitions under subsection (a) shall not
apply to any goods that are the direct product of technology of United States origin under a written agreement
entered into on or before April 20, 1988, and that are
exported prior to the date which is one year after the date
of the enactment of the Anti-Apartheid Act Amendments
of 1989.

"(d) The prohibitions under subsection (a) shall not
apply to—

"(1) economic assistance or human rights programs
for disadvantaged South Africans, South African blacks or
other nonwhite South Africans, or victims of apartheid in
South Africa pursuant to the Foreign Assistance Act of
1961, the Export-Import Bank Act of 1945, or any other
provision of law authorizing economic or human rights
assistance programs; and

"(2) contributions to charitable organizations engaged
in social welfare, public health, religious, educational, and
emergency relief activities in South Africa."

Sec. 103. Repeal of Certain Provisions of the Act;
          Definitions.

(a) Repeal of Certain Provisions of the Act—Effective
180 days after the date of the enactment of this Act, the
Comprehensive Anti-Apartheid Act of 1986 is amended

(1) in title I by striking section 110;

(2) in title II—

(A) by striking sections 207 and 212; and

(B) by redesigning section 211 as section 207;

(3) in title III—

(A) by striking sections 304, 309, 310, 317, 318, 319,
320, 321, and 323;

(B) by redesignating section 315 as section 309; and

(C) by redesignating section 316 as section 310.

(b) Definitions—

(1) Paragraphs (3) and (4) or section 3 of the Act are amended to read as follows:

"(3) the term 'investment in South Africa' means—

"(A) a commitment of funds or other assets (in order to earn a financial return) to a South African entity, including—

"(i) a loan or other extension of credit made to a South African entity, or security given for the debts of an entity;

"(ii) the beneficial ownership or control of a share or interest in a South African entity, or of a bond or other debt instrument issued by such an entity; or

"(iii) capital contributions in money or other assets to a South African entity; or

"(B) the control of a South African entity in cases in which subparagraph (A) does not apply;

"(4) the term 'loan'—

"(A) means any transfer or extension of funds or credit on the basis of an obligation to repay, or any assumption or guarantee of the obligation of another to repay an extension of funds or credit, including—

"(i) overdrafts;

"(ii) currency swaps;

"(iii) the purchase of debt or equity securities issued by the Government of South Africa or a South African entity on or after the date of enactment of this Act;

"(iv) the purchase of a loan made by another person;

"(v) the sale of financial assets subject to an agreement to repurchase;

"(vi) a renewal or refinancing whereby funds or credits are transferred or extended to the Government of South Africa or a South African entity;

"(vii) short-term trade financing, as by letters of credit or similar trade credits;

"(viii) sales on open account in cases where such sales are normal business practices; and

"(ix) rescheduling of existing loans; and

"(B) does not include, a loan for which an agreement was entered into before April 20, 1988, so long as such a loan is maintained under the terms in effect on such date;"

(2) Section 3 of the Act is further amended by—

(A) striking "and" after the semicolon in paragraph (8)(B);

(B) striking the period at the end of paragraph (9) and inserting a semicolon; and

(C) adding at the end of such section the following:

"(10) the terms 'United States person' and 'person subject to the jurisdiction of the Untied States' mean—

"(A) any person, wherever located, who is a citizen or resident of the United States;

"(B) any person actually within the United States;

"(C) any entity organized under the laws of the Untied States or of any State, territory, possession, or district of the Untied States; and

"(D) any partnership, association, corporation, or other organization, wherever organized or doing business, that is owned or controlled by persons specified in subparagraphs (A), (B), or (C) of this paragraph;

"(11) the terms 'goods' and 'technology' have the meanings given such terms by section 16 of the Export Administration Act of 1979;

"(12) the term 'goods subject to the jurisdiction of the United States' includes goods that are the direct product of technology of United States origin; and

"(13) the term 'foreign person'—

"(A) means any person who is not a United States person or subject to the jurisdiction of the United States, and

"(B) does not include any government or any agency or other entity or instrumentality thereof (including a government-sponsored agency) unless any such agency, entity, or instrumentality is a business enterprise."

(3) The amendments made by this subsection shall take effect 180 days after the date of the enactment of this Act.

Sec. 104. Prohibition on United States Intelligence and Military Cooperation With South Africa

(a) Amendment to Comprehensive Anti-Apartheid Act of 1986. The Act is amended by striking section 322 an adding after section 303 the following new section:

"Prohibition on United States Intelligence and Military Cooperation With South Africa

"Sect. 304. (a)(1) No agency or entity of the United States involved in intelligence activities may engage in any form of cooperation, direct or indirect, with the Government of South Africa (specifically including the authorities administering Namibia so long as Namibia is illegally occupied).

"(2) The prohibition under paragraph (1) may not be construed to affect the collection of intelligence under any circumstances which do not involve any form of cooperation, direct or indirect, with the Government of South Africa.

"(b) No agency or entity of the United States may engage in any form of cooperation, direct or indirect, with the armed forces of the Government of South Africa.

"(c) The prohibitions of this section shall not apply to the conduct of diplomatic activities or to intelligence information concerning the military activities or equipment in southern Africa of Cuban military forces or of another Communist country acting in concert with Cuban military forces.

"(d) Funds authorized to be appropriated or otherwise made available by the Congress (including funds specified in an classified schedule of authorizations or appropriations) may not be obligated or expended by any agency or entity of the United States for any expenses related to any cooperation prohibited by this section.

"(e) Consistent with the objectives of this section it is the sense of the Congress that the President should not—

"(1) assign or detail any member of the United States Armed Forces to serve as, or otherwise perform the functions of, a defense (or military) attache in South Africa; or

"(2) accredit any individual to serve as, or otherwise perform the functions of, a defense (or military) attache at a South African diplomatic mission in the Untied States."

(b) Amendment to Intelligence Authorization Act for Fiscal Year 1987—Section 107 of the Intelligence Authorization Act for Fiscal Year 1987 (Public Law 990-569) is hereby repealed.

Sec. 105. Prohibition on Nuclear Assistance to South Africa.

Section 307 of the Act is amended to read as follows: "Prohibition on Nuclear Assistance to South Africa

"Sec. 307. Notwithstanding any other provision of law, the Secretary of Energy shall not, under section 37 b. (2) of the Atomic Energy Act of 1954, authorize any person to engage, directly or indirectly, in the production of special nuclear material in South Africa."

Sec. 106. Independence of Namibia.

(a) Additional Measure for Termination of Certain Provisions of the Act—Section 311 of the Act is amended—

(1) in subsection (a)—

(A) by inserting "402(a)," before "501(c)" in the matter preceding paragraph (1),

(B) in paragraph (4) by striking "and" after the semicolon,

(C) in paragraph (5) by striking the period and inserting "; and", and

(D) by adding after paragraph (5) the following new paragraph:

"(6) ends the illegal occupation of Namibia and implements United Nations Resolution 435 which calls for the independence of Namibia."; and

(2) in subsection (b)—

(A) by inserting "402(a)," before "501(c)", and

(B) by amending paragraph (2) to read as follows:

"(2) taken four of the five actions listed in paragraphs (2) through (6) of subsection (a), and".

(b) Policy Toward the Government of South Africa— Section 101(b) is amended—

(1) in paragraph (5) by striking "and" after the semicolon;

(2) by striking the period at the end of paragraph (6) and inserting "; and"; and

(3) by adding after paragraph (6) the following new paragraph (7):

"(7) end South Africa's illegal occupation of Namibia and implement United Nations Resolution 435 which calls for the establishment of an independent Namibia."

Sec. 107. Penalties.

(a) General Provision—Section 603(b) of the Act is amended to read as follows:

"(b) Except as otherwise provided in this section—

"(1) any person that violates the provisions of this act, or any regulation, license, or order issued to carry out this Act shall be subject to a civil penalty of $50,000;

"(2)(A) any person, other than an individual, that willfully violates the provisions of this Act, or any regulation, license, or order issued to carry out this Act shall be fined not more than $1,000,000;

"(B) any person, other than an individual, that knowingly violates the provisions of this Act, or any regulation, license, or order issued to carry out this Act shall be fined in accordance with title 18, United States Code;

"(3)(A) any individual who willfully violates the provisions of this Act or any regulation, license, or other issued to carry out this Act shall be imprisoned not more than 10 years, fined in accordance with title 18, United States Code, or both;

"(B) any individual who knowingly violates the provisions of this Act, or any regulation, license, or order issued to carry out this Act shall be imprisoned not more than 5 years, fined in accordance with title 18, United States Code, or both; and

"(4) any individual who violates section 302(d)(1) or any regulations issued to carry out that section shall be fined in accordance with title 18, United States Code."

(b) Other Penalties—Section 603(c) of the Act is amended—

(10 in paragraph (1) by striking "not more than $10,000," and inserting "in accordance with title 18, United States Code,"; and

(2) in paragraph (2) by striking "section 301(a)" and inserting "section 302(d)(1)".

(c) Effective Date—The amendments made by this section shall take effect 180 days after the date of the enactment of this Act.

Sec. 108. Coordinator of South Africa Sanctions; Interagency Coordinating Committee on South Africa.

This Act is amended by adding after section 606 the following new sections:

"Coordinator of South Africa Sanctions

"Sec. 6707. (a) There is established within the Department of State a coordinator of South Africa sanctions who shall be responsible to the Secretary of State for matters pertaining to the implementation of sanctions against South Africa, in accordance with the provisions of this section.

"(b) The Secretary of State, through the coordinator of South Africa sanctions, shall—

"(1) lead and coordinate all executive agency activities concerning monitoring of compliance with, and enforcement of, this Act;

"(2) lead and coordinate monitoring by appropriate executive agencies of other countries' trade and financial flows with South Africa (including economic relations which may undermine the effects of United States sanctions);

"(3) assist the Department of Commerce, the Department of the Treasury, and appropriate intelligence and other agencies in carrying out the functions of such agencies under paragraphs (1) and (2); and

"(4) annually prepare and submit, on February 1 of each year after 1990, a comprehensive report to the Congress which—

"(A) describes specific actions taken during the preceding year by each affected executive agency to monitor compliance with, and enforce, the provisions of this Act;

"(B) describes the trade and financial flows (by commodity, activity, total volume, and value) during the preceding year between South Africa and each of its trading and financial partners, including economic relations which may be subject to penalties under section 402;

"(C) including the information required under section 402(b)(3);

"(D) describes the resources utilized by the coordinator, the Department of State, and other executive agencies in carrying out their functions under this Act in the preceding year, including an evaluation of whether such resources were adequate; and

"(E) provides any recommendations of the Secretary of State for improving the effectiveness of the coordinator.

"(c) In carrying out the functions under subsection (b), the coordinator shall place particular emphasis on activities related to strategically important trade in oil, coal, computers, specialized machinery and arms, and to financial credits.

"Interagency Coordinating Committee on South Africa

"Sec. 608. (a) There is established an Interagency Coordinating Committee on South Africa. The Committee shall coordinate and monitor implementation of this Act.

"(b) The committee shall be composed of—

"(1) the Secretary of State,

"(2) the Secretary of the Treasury,

"(3) the Secretary of Defense,

"(4) the Secretary of Commerce,

"(5) the Secretary of Agriculture,

"(6) the Attorney General,

"(7) the United States Trade Representative, and

"(8) such other heads of executive agencies with functions under this Act as the President considers appropriate.

The Secretary of State shall be the chairperson of the Committee."

Sec. 109. Measures to Assist Victims of Apartheid.

(a) Expanding Participation in the South African Economy—Section 203 of the Act is amended—

(1) by striking subsection (b);

(2) in subsection (c) by striking "50" and inserting "90"; and

(3) by redesignating subsection (c) as subsection "(b)".

(b) Export-Import Bank of United States—Effective October 1, 1990, section 2(b)(9)(B) of the Export Import Bank Act of 1945 is amended by striking "majority owned" both places it appears and inserting "90 percent owned and controlled."

(c) Code of Conduct—

(1) Section 208 of the Act is amended—

(A) by striking subsections (b), (c), (d), and (e);

(B) by striking "(a)" after the section designation; and
(C) by striking "sections 203, 205, 207, and 603" and
inserting section 205".

(2) Section 603 of the Act is amended by striking
subsection (d).

(d) Effective Date—The provisions of this section
shall take effect 180 days after the date of the enactment
of this Act.

Sec. 110. Assistance for disadvantaged South Africans.

(a) Amendment to Foreign Assistance Act of 1961—
Section 535(a) of the Foreign Assistance Act of 1961 is
amended

(1) by amending paragraph (1) to read as follows:

"Sec. 535. Economic Support for Disadvantaged South
Africans—(a)(1) Up to $40,000,000 of the funds author-
ized to be appropriated to carry out this chapter and any
other economic development assistance activities under
the Foreign Assistance Act of 1961, for the fiscal year 1990
and each fiscal year thereafter, shall be available for assistance for disadvantaged South Africans. Assistance under
this section shall be provided for activities that are consistent with the objective of a majority of South Africans for
an end to the apartheid system and the establishment of
a society based on nonracial principles. Such activities
may include scholarships (including scholarships for study
in the health care professions and the health sciences),
assistance to promote the participation of disadvantaged
South Africans in trade unions and private enterprise, alternative education and community development programs, and training and other assistance (including legal
aid in challenging government media restrictions) for
South African journalists."

(2) in paragraph (2) by striking "programs for South
Africa's trade unionists." and inserting "and other support

programs (including legal assistance) for trade unions in South Africa and Namibia, including COSATU (Congress of South African Trade Unions), NACTU (National Council of Trade Unions), and NUNW (National Union of Namibian Workers), their affiliates, and other viable unions in order to develop a balanced assistance program which is representative of the trade union movement." and

(3) by adding after paragraph (2) the following new paragraph:

"(3) not less than $4,000,000 of the amounts provided for each fiscal year pursuant to this subsection shall be available for programs of refugee education and assistance for South Africans and Namibians."

(b) Effective Date—The amendments made by subsection (a) shall take effect October 1, 1989.

Sec. 111. Restrictions regarding involvement in the South African Energy Sector.

(a) Restrictions Regarding Involvement in the South African Energy Sector—The Act is amended by adding after section 314 the following new section 315:

"Sec. 315. (a) A United States person may not, directly or through an affiliate, provide transport to South Africa of a commercial quantity of crude oil or refined petroleum products. The prohibition under this subsection includes transport on a vessel of United States registry and transport on a vessel owned, directly or indirectly, by a United States person.

"(b)(1) Effective 180 days after the date of the enactment of this subsection, the Secretary of the Interior may not issue any lease pursuant to the Mineral Leasing Act of 1920, the Mineral Leasing Act for Acquired Lands, the Outer Continental Shelf Lands Act, or the Geothermal Steam Act of 1970 to any national of the United States which is controlled by, or under common control with, any foreign person who—

"(A) purchases, acquires, owns, or holds any investment in South Africa; or

"(B) exports to South Africa, directly or indirectly,
any crude oil or refined petroleum products.

"(2) Prior to issuing any lease referred to in paragraph (1), the Secretary of the Interior shall require an
applicant for such a lease to certify that the applicant is
not subject to the provisions of paragraph (1)."

(b) Waiver of Prohibition on Issuance of Leases—A
person affected by the prohibition under section 315(b) of
the Comprehensive Anti-Apartheid Act of 1986 (as
amended by subsection (a)) may apply to the President for
a one-time waiver of the prohibition. With respect to any
applicant, the President may waive the application of
section 315(b) for not more than 180 days after such
subsection takes effect. Such waiver may be granted only
for good cause.

Part B—Policy Statements; Reports; Studies; and Other-
    Miscellaneous Provisions

    Sec. 121. Sense of Congress Regarding Antitrust
    Investigation of South African Diamond Cartel,
    Study of Diamond Origins, and Enforcement of
    Prohibition on Importation of South African
    Diamonds into the United States.

It is the sense of the Congress that—
(1) the President should direct the Attorney General
of the United States to conduct an investigation of the
South African-controlled international diamond cartel in
order to ascertain if any enforcement action is appropriate
under the antitrust laws of the Untied States;

(2) the President should direct the Secretary of
Commerce and the Commissioner of Customs to conduct
a study to determine the feasibility of identifying at port
of entry, without harm to producers and processors of

diamonds outside of South Africa, the national origin of diamonds entering the United States; and

(3) the President should—

(A) ensure effective and rigorous enforcement of a prohibition on the importation into the United States of uncut diamonds of South African origin by—

(i) applying direct pressure on the Central Selling Organization in London to identify and segregate diamonds by country of origin and encouraging other nations (including diamond-producing nations) to take appropriate measure to achieve that result; and

(ii) entering into negotiations for agreements with the principal exporting nations of uncut diamonds to the United States (particularly the United Kingdom and Switzerland) to ensure that uncut South African diamonds will not be exported to the United States;

(b) pursue effective enforcement and undertake appropriate actions to obtain the identification and segregation of uncut diamonds of South African origin, provided such enforcement and other actions do not interfere with the ability of United States importers to import uncut diamonds of other countries of origin despite any unknowing importation of unidentified uncut South African diamonds which may occur; and

(C) direct the Secretary of the Treasury to submit a report on the status of the effort to identify and segregate uncut South African diamonds to the Speaker of the House of Representatives and the President of the Senate 180 days after the date of the enactment of this Act and every 180 days thereafter.

Sec. 122. Sense of Congress Regarding South African Consulates and Approval of Visas.

It is the sense of the Congress that—

(1) South Africa has effectively banned 19 major anti-

apartheid organizations, forbade the major trade union federation, COSATU, from engaging in political activities, and denied permission for travel to the United States to numerous South Africans;

(2) the repression by South Africa of domestic and foreign media has prevented the free flow of information essential to the advance of any national dialogue between the government and the nonwhite majority which actively opposes apartheid, and has restricted the ability of the foreign press to report developments in South Africa;

(3) the President should immediately close two of South Africa's consulates general, eliminate all honorary consuls which South Africa has in the United States, and forbid South Africa to expand the staffing of its embassy beyond the level of January 1, 1988; and

(4) approval of temporary United States visas, especially to South African government personnel, should be granted on a case-by-case basis only after close scrutiny of the South African Government's record of allowing South African citizens, particularly those who are members of anti-apartheid organizations, to travel to the United States.

Sec. 123. Study of Measures to Reduce South Africa's Foreign Exchange Earnings From Gold.

(a) Study—In consultation with other industrialized nations and international financial institutions, the President shall conduct a study of possible actions by the United States to reduce the foreign exchange earnings of South Africa which accrue through sales of gold. The President shall consider possible international and domestic consequences of any course of action and shall evaluate mechanisms to avoid or minimize any adverse effects on the United States gold mining industry.

(b) Report—Not later than 180 days after the date of

the enactment of this Act, the President shall submit to the Congress a report of the findings of such study.

Sec. 124. Report on South Africa's Involvement in International Terrorism.

Not less than 90 days after the date of the enactment of this Act, the Secretary of State shall prepare and submit a detailed report to the Committee on Foreign Affairs of the House of Representatives and the Committee on Foreign Relations of the Senate concerning the extent to which the Government of South Africa has been involved in or has provided support for acts of international terrorism.

TITLE II—SANCTIONS AGAINST SOUTH AFRICAN IMPORTS INTO THE UNITED STATES

Sec. 201. Prohibitions on imports from South Africa.

(a) Prohibition on Imports—Effective 180 days after the date of the enactment of this Act, section 302 of the Act is amended to read as follows:

"Prohibition on Imports Into the United States From South Africa.

"Sec. 302. (a) No article which is grown, produced, extracted, or manufactured in South Africa may be imported into the United States.

"(b) The prohibition of subsection (a) shall not apply to the import of—

"(1) any strategic mineral (including any ferroalloy thereof) with respect to which the President certifies to the Congress for purposes of this Act that the quantities of such mineral which are essential for the economy, public health, or defense of the United States are not available from alternative reliable suppliers; and

"(2) publications, including books, newspapers, magazines, films, television programming, phonograph records, video and audio tape recordings, photographs, microfilm, microfiches, posters, and similar materials.

"(c) The prohibition under subsection (a) shall not apply to imports from business enterprises in South Africa that are wholly-owned by persons economically and politically disadvantaged by apartheid.

"(d) The prohibition under subsection (a) includes—

"(1) South African krugerrands or any other gold coin minted in South Africa or offered by sale by the Government of South Africa;

"(2) uranium hexafluoride that has been manufactured from South African uranium or uranium oxide; and

"(3) fish or seafood—

"(A) purchased from a ship owned by a South African or of South African registry.

"(B) purchased from a South African,

"(C) processed in whole or part by a South African ship or person, or

"(D) stored in or shipped from South Africa."

(b) Certification—The certification of the President with respect to any strategic mineral under section 303(a)(2) of the Comprehensive Anti-Apartheid Act of 1986 (as in effect prior to the date of the enactment of this Act) shall be effective for purposes of section 302(b)(1) of such Act as amended by this Act, unless the President rescinds or modifies such a certification.

Sec. 202. Multilateral Measures, Including Import Restrictions, to Dismantle Apartheid.

(a) Negotiating Authority —Section 401(b) of the Act is amended to read as follows:

"(b)(1) The President, or at his direction, the Secretary of State (in consultation with the United States Trade Representative), shall, consistent with the policy under subsection (a), confer with the other industrialized democracies in order to reach cooperative agreements to impose sanctions against South Africa to bring about the complete dismantling of apartheid.

"(2) Before the 180th day after the date of the enactment of the Anti-Apartheid Act Amendments of 1989, the President shall submit a report to the Congress containing

"(A) a description of United States efforts under paragraph (1) to implement multilateral measures to bring about the complete dismantling of apartheid;

"(B) his evaluation regarding whether the efforts described in subparagraph (A) have been successful in achieving multilateral measures to bring about the complete dismantling of apartheid; and

"(C) if the efforts described in subparagraph (A) have been successful, a detailed description of economic and other measures adopted by the other industrialized countries to bring about the complete dismantling of apartheid, including an assessment of the stringency with which such measures are enforced by those countries."

(b) United Nations Sanctions—Section 401(e) of the Act is amended by striking "It is the sense of the Congress that the President should" and inserting "The President shall".

(c) Limitation on Imports From and Contracting With Certain Foreign Persons—Section 402 of the Act is amended to read a follows:

"Limitation on Imports From and Contracting With Certain Foreign Persons

"Sec. 402. (a)(1) Subject to subsection (b), effective on and after the 180th-day after the date of the enactment of the Anti-Apartheid Act Amendments of 1989 (or the 360th day after such date if the evaluation of the President under section 401(b)(2)(B) is affirmative), to the extent that a foreign person takes significant commercial advantage of any sanction or prohibition imposed by or under this Act, the President shall impose not less than one of the penalties under paragraph (2).

"(2) The President may impose one or both of the following penalties under paragraph (1):

"(A) Limit the importation into the United States of any product or service of the foreign person.

"(B) Restrict the foreign person from contracting with departments, agencies, and instrumentalities of the United States Government.

"(3) For purposes of applying this subsection—

"(A) the European Community shall be treated as being a single industrialized democracy; and

"(B) any limitation imposed under paragraph (2)(A) shall, to the extend possible, offset the value of the significant commercial advantage obtained by the foreign person.

"(b)(1) The President may waive the application of subsection (a) with respect to foreign persons of an industrialized democracy that is party an agreement that has entered into force with respect to the United States under section 401.

"(2) The President shall revoke, for such time and subject to such conditions as he considers appropriate, a waiver made under paragraph (1) if the President finds that the industrialized democracy that is party to the agreement in force under section 401 is not adequately enforcing the measures provided for under the agreement.

"(3) The annual report required under section 607(b)(4) shall include, with respect to the period covered by the report—

"(A) an evaluation of the extent to which the import restrictions, if any, provided for under each agreement in force under section 401 are being enforced by the industrialized democracy concerned and the effect of such enforcement; and

"(B) the reasons for each waiver and revocation made under paragraphs (1) and (2)."

Sec. 203. Referral in the House of Joint Resolutions Pertaining to Import Restrictions.

Section 602(a)(2) of the Act is amended to read as follows:
"(2)(A) A joint resolution, other than a joint resolution referred to in subparagraph (B), shall, upon introduction, be referred to the Committee on Foreign Affairs of the House of Representatives.

"(B) A joint resolution under—
"(i) section 311(b), if the joint resolution suspends or modifies any import restriction in effect under   title III, section 402(a), 501(c), or 504(b);
"(ii) section 401(d), if the joint resolution approves an agreement encompassing any import restriction measure; or
"(iii) section 501(d), if the joint resolution would enact any import restriction under section 501(c); shall, upon introduction, be jointly referred to the Committee on Foreign Affairs and the Committee on Ways and Means of the House of Representatives."

Sec. 204. Reports on United States Imports From Member States of the Council for Mutual Economic Assistance.

Section 502 of the Act is amended to read as follows:
"Reports on United States Imports From Member States of the Council for Mutual Economic Assistance
"Sec. 502. Beginning 30 days after the date of the enactment of the Anti-Apartheid Act Amendments of 1989, and every 30 days thereafter, the President, through the Secretary of Commerce, shall prepare and transmit to the Congress a report setting for the average amounts of imports of coal or any strategic and critical material entering the United States from each member country and

observer country of the Council for Mutual Economic Assistance (C.M.E.A.)"

Sec. 205. Program to Reduce Dependence Upon Importation of Strategic Minerals From South Africa.

Section 504(b) of the Act is amended to read as follows:

"(b)(1) The President shall develop a program to reduce the dependence, if any, of the United States on the importation from South Africa of the materials identified in the report submitted under subsection (a). In the development of such program, the President shall determine (in consultation with knowledgeable individuals in industry, government, and academia) whether, to what extent, and in what time period, adequate quantities of such materials could reasonably be obtained from (A) alternative reliable domestic and foreign sources, and (B) improved and effective methods of manufacturing, substitution, conservation, recovery, and recycling. Such determination shall include consideration of the quality and cost of such materials.

"(2) Not more than 270 days after the date of the enactment of the Anti-Apartheid Act Amendments of 1989, the President shall submit to Congress concerning the program under paragraph (1), particularly the respective roles in the implementation of such program of the Federal Government, users of such materials, and other affected persons. On February 1, 1991, and on February 1 of each subsequent year until the termination of sanctions under this Act, the President shall submit a report to the Congress concerning progress in implementing such program."

Sec. 206. Preventing circumvention of United States Import Restrictions.

Within 180 days after the date of the enactment of

this Act and at such times thereafter as are appropriate, the President, or the designee of the President, shall confer with the governments of the African "frontline" states regarding the content and implementation of appropriate measures to prevent the circumvention by South Africa of the import restrictions on South African products placed in effect by the United States under the authority of this Act.

TITLE III—GENERAL PROVISIONS

Sec. 301. Technical and Conforming Amendments.

(a) Amendments to the Table of Contents—
(1) Section 2 of the Act relating to the table of contents for title III is amended to read as follows:

"Title III—Measures by the United States to Undermine Apartheid

"Sec. 301. Prohibition on investment in South Africa.
"Sec. 302. Prohibition on imports into the United States from South Africa.
"Sec. 303. Prohibition of exports to South Africa from the United States.
"Sec. 304. Prohibition on United States intelligence and military cooperation with South Africa.
Restrictions regarding involvement in the South African energy sector.
"Sec. 305. Prohibitions on loans to the Government of South Africa.
"Sec. 306. Prohibition on air transportation with South Africa.
Sec. 307. Prohibition on nuclear assistance to South Africa.
"Sec. 308. Government of South Africa bank accounts.
"Sec. 309. Prohibition on the promotion of United States tourism in South Africa.

"Sec. 310. Prohibition on United States Government assistance to, involvement in, or subsidy for trade with, South Africa.

"Sec. 311. Termination of certain provisions.

"Sec. 312. Policy toward violence or terrorism.

"Sec. 313. Termination of tax treaty and protocol.

"Sec. 314. Prohibition of United States Government procurement from South Africa.

"Sec. 315. Restrictions regarding involvement in the South African energy sector."

(2) The table of contents in section 2 of the Act is further amended—

(A) by amending the item relating to section 207 to read as follows:

"Sec. 207. Prohibition on assistance to any person or group engaging in 'necklacing'."

(B) by striking the item relating to section 212;

(C) by amending the items relating to sections 402 and 502, respectively, to read as follows:

"Sec. 402. Limitation on imports from and contracting with certain foreign persons.

"Sec. 502. Reports on United States imports from member states of the Council for Mutual Economic Assistance." and

(D) by adding after the item relating to section ;606 the following items:

"Sec. 607. Coordinator of South Africa sanctions.

"Sec. 608. Interagency coordinating committee on South Africa."

(b) Conforming Amendments to the Act—

(1) Section 602(a)(1) and 602(b)(1) of the Act are amended by striking "318(b),"

(2) Section 602(c) is amended by striking paragraph (2) and redesignating paragraphs "(3)" and "(4)" as paragraphs "(2)" and "(3)", respectively.

(3) Section 501(c) of the Act is amended—

(A) by inserting "or other measures" after "additional measures"; and

(B)(i) by striking paragraphs (2) and (4);

(ii) by inserting "and" at the end of paragraph (1);

(iii) by striking "; and" and inserting in lieu thereof a period at the end of paragraph (3); and

(iv) by redesignating paragraph (3) as paragraph "(2)".

(c) Effective Date—The amendments made by this section shall take effect 180 days after the date of the enactment of this Act.

Sec. 302. Effective Date.

Except as otherwise provided, this Act and the amendments made by this Act shall take effect on the date of the enactment of this Act.

Appendix B

Carnegie Endowment for International Peace

2400 N Street, NW, Washington, DC 20037

Introduction

The Carnegie Endowment professional staff consists of Senior Associates and Resident Associates who bring to their work substantial first-hand experience in foreign affairs. Their backgrounds include government, journalism and public affairs, including significant overseas service. Current Endowment staff and projects, which are identified in this brochure, cover a broad range of contemporary policy issues—military, political and economic. Through writing, public and media appearances, and participation in programs at our Conference Center, our staff engages the major policy issues of the day in ways that reach both expert and general audiences. Through periodic staff and project changes, we continue to orient our projects to timely and important subjects and to facilitate work under the Endowment's auspices by diverse foreign policy professionals.

Thomas L. Hughes
President

Shirley M. Hufstedler
Partner, Hufstedler, Miller, Kaus & Beardsley
Thomas L. Hughes
President, Carnegie Endowment for International Peace
Wilbert J. LeMelle
President Mercy College
Stephen R. Lewis, Jr.
President, Carlton College
George N. Lindsay
Senior Partner, Debevoise & Plimpton
George C. Lodge
Professor of Business Administration,Harvard University Graduate School of Business Administration
William B. Macomber
Retired President, Metropolitan Museum of Art
Newton N. Minow
Partner, Sidley & Austin
Barbara W. Newell
Regents Professor, Florida State University
William J. Perry
Chairman, H&Q Technology Partners Inc.
Wesley W. Posvar
President, University of Pittsburgh
Edson W. Spencer
Chairman, Spencer Associates
Strobe Talbott
Editor-at-Large, Time Magazine
Charles J. Zwick
Chairman, Southeast Banking Corporation

Staff and Projects

Jose E. Alvarez, Resident Associate
International Law & Organizations
Policy and legal considerations regarding operation of

international organizations in the US . . . respective roles of the Executive Branch and the Congress . . . issues relating to UN financing and to privileges and immunities.

International Affairs Fellow, Council on Foreign Relations; Associate Professor, George Washington University, National Law Center; Attorney-Adviser, Office of the Legal Adviser, US Department of State; Attorney, Shea & Gardner, Washington, DC.

Pauline H. Baker, Senior Associate
US Policy Toward Africa

Evolution of US-Africa policy . . . implications for the West of Africa's current economic crisis . . . strategic and political developments in southern Africa . . . prospects for fundamental change in South Africa.

Research Scientist, Battelle Memorial Institute; Professional Staff Member, US Senate Foreign Relations Committee; Rockefeller Foundation Fellow; Lecturer, University of Lagos, Nigeria.

Nayan Chanda, Senior Associate
Major Powers & Southeast Asia

Peace negotiations on Cambodia . . . the Khmer Rouge and national reconciliation . . . US relations with Vietnam and Southeast Asia . . . Soviet policy toward Southeast Asia . . . ASEAN and Indochinese relations with China.

Washington Correspondent, Indochina Correspondent of the *Far Eastern Economic Review*; Visiting Fellow, Australian National University, Canberra; author of *Brother Enemy: The War After the War, A History of Indochina Since the Fall of Saigon*.

Gregory Flynn, Senior Associate
Strategic Issues & US Alliance Relationships

Continuity and change in the strategic debate . . . role of allies and alliances in US global policy . . . the domestic contexts for allied strategic discourse . . . implications of US-Soviet relations for the Western security debate.

Deputy Director and Assistant Director, Atlantic Institute for International Affairs; Graduate Research Fellow, Program for Science and International Affairs, Harvard University; Special Assistant to the Executive Director, Center for European Studies, Harvard University.

Gillian Gunn, Senior Associate
Cuban Foreign Policy

Cuba and the Angola/Namibia negotiations and implications for other regional conflicts . . . impact of new Soviet policies upon Cuban foreign policy options . . . external and domestic factors in Cuban foreign policy . . . US-Cuban relations.

Fellow, African Studies Program, Center for Strategic and International Studies; International Relations Fellow, Rockefeller Foundation; Africa Editor and Assistant Editor, Business International, London; Senior Editor for Africa and Latin America, *World Times* Magazine, London.

Daniel S. Hamilton, Senior Associate
The Two Germanies & the Future of Europe

Political, economic, and security issues in German-American relations . . . *glasnost* and prospects for reform in the GDR . . . Germany's role in Gorbachev's "Common European House" . . . Germany, the US, and the European Community after 1992.

Deputy Director, Aspen Institute Berlin; Lecturer in US Foreign Policy, Free University of Berlin; Washington Consultant and Program Officer, The Chicago Council on Foreign Relations; Dean, Concordia College "total immersion" German Language Village.

Selig S. Harrison, Senior Associate
South & East Asia

India-Pakistan relations . . . Pakistan, Afghanistan and impact of Soviet occupation . . . Indian Ocean geopolitics . . . Sino-American and Japanese-American relations . . . South Korean politics and South Korean-North Korean relations.

Author of five books on Asian affairs and US policy problems in Asia; Washington Post Bureau Chief in New Delhi and Tokyo; Managing Editor, *The New Republic*; Senior Fellow in charge of Asian studies, Brookings Institution.

Geoffrey Kemp, Senior Associate
Arms Control & Proliferation in the Near East & South Asia
Impact of nuclear, chemical, missile and conventional weapons on regional conflict . . . prospects for limiting the dangers through more stringent supplier and recipient constraints . . . perspectives on regional arms control arrangements.

Senior Fellow, CSIS, Georgetown University; Special Assistant to the President for National Security Affairs; Associate Professor of International Politics, Fletcher School of Law and Diplomacy, Tufts University; Consultant, US Senate Committee on Foreign Relations and US Department of Defense.

Paul H. Kreisberg, Senior Associate
American Policy in Asia
US relations with Asian states from Pakistan to Japan . . . political and economic change in Asia . . . US-Soviet strategic competition in East, Southeast and South Asia.

Director of Studies, Council on Foreign Relations; Career Foreign Service Officer; Deputy Director, Department of State Policy Planning Staff; Political Counselor, American Embassy, New Delhi.

Doris M. Meissner, Senior Associate
Immigration & US Foreign Policy

US immigration and refugee issues . . . international migration developments and US foreign policy . . . problems of illegal immigration to the US and policy responses. Executive Associate Commissioner, US Immigration & Naturalization Service (INS); Acting Commissioner, INS; Deputy Associate Attorney General, US Department of Justice; White House Fellow.

Daniel N. Nelson, Senior Associate
Nato-Warsaw Pact Relations

Evolving security problems inside the Warsaw Pact . . . Moscow-Warsaw-East Berlin military relationships . . . growing political differentiation in Eastern Europe . . . implications for the United States and the Western alliance.

Professor of Political Science, University of Kentucky; Kellogg Foundation National Fellow; author of *Understanding Communism; Romanian Politics in the Ceausescu Era; Elite-Mass Relations in Communist Systems.*

Andrew J. Pierre, Senior Associate
European-American & East-West Relations

"1992" and West European integration . . . the trans-Atlantic connection and the transformation of NATO . . . disintegration of the Soviet bloc and the Western response to *perestroika* . . . towards a pan-European order.

Director-General, Atlantic Institute for International Affairs; Senior Fellow and Director, Project on European-American Relations, Council on Foreign Relations; Brookings Institution and Hudson Institute; Foreign Service Officer; author, *The Global Politics of Arms Sales.*

Tina Rosenberg, Resident Associate
Latin America

Political violence in Latin America . . . public and private terrorism . . . problems in democratization and in the promotion of human rights . . . strengthening judicial systems and rule of law . . . US policy toward Latin America.

MacArthur Fellow; Freelance journalist in Latin America for US magazines and newspapers; author of forthcoming book on violence in Latin America.

David J. Scheffer, Senior Associate
International & National Security Law

Current developments in international and national security law . . . US-Soviet approaches to international law . . . UN and World Court affairs . . . role of law in US foreign policy . . . legal issues in export controls and intelligence oversight.

Staff Consultant, Committee on Foreign Affairs, US House of Representatives; Adjunct Professor, Columbia University; Research Associate, Center for International Affairs, Harvard University; Associate Attorney, Coudert Brothers (New York and Singapore).

David K. Shipler, Senior Associate
Democratization & US Foreign Policy

Democratic evolution in authoritarian states . . . *glasnost* and *perestroika* in the Soviet political system . . . the American role in encouraging or inhibiting democratization in the Third World . . . human rights as a factor in US foreign policy.

Pulitzer-prize winning author of *Arab and Jew: Wounded Spirits in a Promised Land; Russia; Broken Idols, Solemn Dreams*; Chief Diplomatic Correspondent, Jerusalem Bureau Chief, Moscow Bureau Chief, Saigon Correspondent, *New York Times*; Guest Scholar, Brookings Institution.

Dimitri K. Simes, Senior Associate
Soviet Foreign Policy

Soviet foreign policy formulation, world outlook and policies toward the US, Europe, and the Middle East . . .

Soviet military power, strategy, attitudes toward arms control . . . domestic sources of Soviet policy.

Research Professor and Director, Soviet and East European Research Program, SAIS, Johns Hopkins University; Director, Soviet Studies, CSIS, Georgetown University; author of *Detent and Conflict: Soviet Foreign Policy, 1972-1977*.

Leonard S. Spector, Senior Associate
Nuclear Non-Proliferation

Curbing the spread of nuclear arms to additional nations . . . nuclear energy in the developing world . . . nuclear technology export controls . . . multilateral non-proliferation institutions.

Chief Counsel, Energy and Nuclear Proliferation Subcommittee, US Senate; Special Counsel to a Nuclear Regulatory Commissioner.

Melor G. Sturua, Senior Associate
Evolving Soviet-American Relations

The foundations and rationale for a positive evolution of Soviet-American relations . . . opportunities and obstacles . . . prospects for the negotiations in Geneva and Vienna. . . . Soviet and American approach toward the idea of a "Common European House."

Bureau Chief, Foreign Editor and Political Columnist *Izvestia*, including assignments in London, New York and Washington, DC; Member, Union of Soviet Journalists, and the Writer's Union of the USSR; Member, Board of Directors of the Soviet-American Friendship Society.

Viron P. Vaky, Senior Associate
Inter-American System & Regional Governance

Evolution of Inter-American institutions . . . major policy issues on the hemispheric agenda for the future . . . multilateral diplomacy . . . Andean Countries . . . US-Latin American policy.

Research Professor in Diplomacy, Georgetown University; Career Foreign Service Officer; US Assistant Secretary of State; US Ambassador to Venezuela, Colombia and Costa Rica.

Staff—Virginia Babin, Bob Bach, Caroline Bahr, Peggy Bailey, James Butler, Kathleen Defty, Noreen D'Souza, Tiffany Farrell, Kristin Fitzgerald, Betsy Hamilton, Sandi Harris, Chris Henley, Jean Hensley, Stacey Hodges, Kate Lusheck, Michael Lalli, Violet Lee, Jane Lowenthal, Lynn Meininger, Ida O'Connell, Toula Papanicolas, Ann-Kristin Ratnavale, Carrie Roy, Yasmin Santiago, Shelley Stahl, Ann Stecker, Alicja Stevenson, Lynde Tracey

Interns—James McKeever, ‚Jennifer Reingold, Matthew Rendall, Geoffrey Ritts, Catherine Rojas, John Schields, Alvaro Tafur, Maurits van der Veen

Special Programs

Face-to-Face, Gilbert Kulick, *Director*

An invitation-only forum to facilitate dialogue among American governmental and nongovernmental participants on major international issues. Speakers participate in informal, off-the-record dinner discussions with a cross-section of key senior and working-level officials of the Executive Branch and Congress, media, business and industry, and institutions and individuals involved in the foreign policy process.

Foreign Policy Press Breakfast Meetings, C. William Maynes, *Editor*

Foreign Policy magazine regularly sponsors on-the-record breakfast meetings in Washington between foreign-policy news makers and the international affairs press. Guest speakers include US and foreign government officials, visiting dignitaries, and journalists.

Mid-Atlantic Club, Thomas L. Hughes, *Chairman*

The Mid-Atlantic Club is jointly sponsored by the European Communities Delegations and the Carnegie Endowment to encourage discussion among private experts, former officials and current representatives of US and European governmental, financial, economic and social organizations. The group meets monthly for an informal luncheon session to hear guest speakers address a broad range of issues affecting US-European relations.

East-West Relations in Europe, Gregory Flynn, *Director*

This study group brings together 25 current and former senior government officials from the Administration, Congress, and the intelligence community, academics, journalists, and businessmen with special interest and expertise in European security issues. Meeting monthly, its purpose is to examine how best to manage European and American differences about appropriate Western response to change in the Soviet Union and Eastern Europe.

Arms Proliferation in the Near East and South Asia Project, Geoffrey Kemp, *Director*

Through regular meetings and a planned international conference on the impact of the arms race on prospects for conflict in the Near East and South Asia, this study group devotes special attention to three topics: the spread of weapons of mass destruction and delivery systems; the policy dilemmas facing the United States in attempting to implement arms control regimes; the different perspectives on arms control of the regional powers and other key suppliers, especially the Soviet Union, China and Europe.

Immigration Policy Project, Doris Meissner, *Director*

Through a program of informational briefings, roundtable

discussions of key policy questions for the 1990's, and published articles and reports, this project brings a growing body of migration research to immigration policy decision-makers. Project staff also provide an independent voice to inform immigration policy debates, focusing particularly upon the international and comparative dimensions of immigration issues.

Inter-American Roundtable Breakfast Meetings, Viron P. Vaky, *Director*

Co-sponsored with the Inter-American Dialogue, this series of breakfast meetings features key government officials, politicians and academic and civic figures from both Latin America and the United States who lead discussions on current issues and problems in inter-American relations. The meetings are shaped primarily for the benefit of the media, Congressional staff and Latin American academic and research centers.

South African Breakfast Meetings, Pauline H. Baker, *Director*

This series of breakfast meetings provides opportunities for the foreign affairs community, including the press, to address issues concerning South Africa. The meetings principally feature guest speakers from South Africa who lead discussions of events and developments affecting US-South African relations and internal trends in the region.

US-Asian Relations Luncheon Meetings, Paul H. Kreisberg & Selig S. Harrison, *Directors*

Endowment Senior Associates specializing in political, economic and security issues relating to Asia meet with scholars, journalists, administration officials and members of Congress and their staffs for informal discussions of critical developments affecting US policy. Distinguished visitors from Asian countries are often special guests.

US-Soviet Relations Study Group, Dimitri K. Simes,
Director

Chaired by former Secretary of Defense and Secretary of
Energy, James Schlesinger, the study group includes 27
current and former senior administration officials, members of both houses of Congress, academics, journalists
and businessmen. Its purpose is to provide a forum for
discussion on change in the Soviet Union and its implications for the United States.

The Western Hemisphere Forum, Viron P. Vaky, *Mod-
erator*

Luncheon meetings for Latin American and Caribbean
ambassadors to the US and the OAS are held monthly.
The Forum provides guests an opportunity to meet with
experts to discuss topics of special interest concerning the
US, its government, society and policies.

Publications

**Commercial Observation Satellites and Interna-
tional Society**, *edited by Michael Krepon, Peter D. Zimmerman, Leonard S. Spector and Mary Umberger*

The availability of improved satellite photography can be
used for many peaceful as well as military applications.
This book is the result of a Carnegie Endowment study of
the international security implications of commercial
observation satellites. Experts in the field suggest beneficial applications and safeguards against misuse. This
project was made possible by a grant from the Carnegie
Corporation of New York. (Published by Macmillan Press)

The Undeclared Bomb, The Spread of Nuclear Weapons 1987-1988, *by Leonard S. Spector*

This book is the fourth in the annual series by the

Endowment's Non-Proliferation Project. The project monitors the spread of nuclear weapons in order to increase public awareness of the proliferation issue and to provide authoritative information for policymakers and the media. *The Undeclared Bomb*—like the first three books in the series, *Nuclear Proliferation Today* (Vintage Books, 1984), *The New Nuclear Nations* (Vintage Books, 1985), and *Going Nuclear* (Ballinger Publishing, 1987)- covers developments in the key emerging nuclear states: Argentina, Brazil, India, Iran, Iraq, Israel, Libya, Pakistan, South Africa, and Taiwan. This project is supported by the Carnegie Corporation of New York and the Rockefeller Brothers Fund. A fifth volume, *Nuclear Ambitions,* is now in preparation. (Published by Ballinger Publishing Company)

Nuclear Weapons and South Asian Security, Report of the Carnegie Task Force on Non-Proliferation and South Asian Security, *Leonard S. Spector, Chairman*

Amidst growing concerns over the intensifying nuclear competition between India and Pakistan, this report published in 1988 examines the prospects for nuclear proliferation in the region and proposes a step-by-step process for slowing this dangerous trend. The Task Force was funded by a project grant from the W. Alton Jones Foundation, Inc., and by grants from the Carnegie Corporation of New York and the Rockefeller Brothers Fund. (Published by the Carnegie Endowment)

Foreign Policy

The quarterly journal *Foreign Policy* was launched in 1970 to encourage fresh debate on the vital issues confronting US foreign policy. It has grown in circulation and prominence and is now respected, cited and watched by American government officials, world leaders, influential figures in corporate and labor circles, and students of foreign relations. *Foreign Policy* is syndicated by the New York Times Syndication Sales Corporation, and its articles have been reprinted and commented upon in newspapers and magazines worldwide.

Editor—C. William Maynes. Mr. Maynes has been a Foreign Service Officer, Secretary of the Carnegie Endowment, and Assistant Secretary of State for International Organizations Affairs.

Staff—Thomas Omestad, Associate Editor; Deborah Chiao, Circulation Director; Stephanie Terry, Copy Editor; Mary Brennan, Production Manager; Julie Reed, Advertising manager

Editorial Board—Thomas L. Hughes, chairman; C. Fred Bergsten, Seweryn Bailer, Frances FitzGerald, Lawrence Freedman, Morton H. Halperin, Stanley Hoffmann, Robert D. Hormats, Karl Kaiser, Jan M. Lodal, Donald F. McHenry, Thierry de Montbrial, Joseph S. Nye, Jr., John E. Rielly, William D. Rogers, Helmut Sonnenfeldt, Tad Szulc, Richard H. Ullman

Former Endowment Professionals

Adolfo Aguilar Zinser, *Mexico-US Relations*
James E. Baker, *South Africa*
Frank C. Ballance, *Congress & the Third World*
Donald K. Bandler, *Face-to-Face*
Robert W. Barnett, *East Asia*
Karl S. Beck, *South & Southern Africa*
Peter D. Bell, *US-Latin American Relations & Development*
Diane B. Bendahmane, *Publications*
C. Fred Bergsten, *International Economics*
David Biltchuk, *Face-to-Face*

Lise Bissonnette, *Quebec-0US Relations*
Barry M. Blechman, *Arms Control & Security*
Andrew Borowiec, *Yugoslavia*
Patrick Breslin, *Latin America*
Robin Broad, *Multilateral Institutions & Development*
Frederick Z. Brown, *US Policy Toward Indochina*
Seyom Brown, *US-Soviet Relations*
Richard Burt, *Arms Control*
Margaret Van W. Carpenter, *The Kurds*
Alexandre Casella, *Southeast Asia*
Jorge G. Castaneda, *US-Mexican Relations*
James Chace, *Ideology& Foreign Policy*
Patrick Cockburn, *Soviet Domestic Developments*
Benjamin J. Cohen, *International Economics*
Evelyn Colbert, *Southeast & East Asia*
John K. Cooley, *North Africa*
Jonathan Dean, *Arms Control in Europe*
T. McAdams DeFord, *Face-to-Face*
Hugh De Santis, *European Security/East-West Relations*
Terry L. Deibel, *US-Third World Security Relationships*
John de St. Jorre, *Southern Africa*
I. M. Destler, *Executive-Congressional Relations*
Kenneth Dillon, *Face-to-Face*
John DiSciullo, *Italy*
Ronald A. Dwight, *Face-to-Face*
Robert J. Einhorn, *Face-to-Face*
Tom J. Farer, *Horn of Africa*
Richard E. Feinberg, *Latin America*
Thomas M. Franck, *International Law*
Lawrence G. Franko, *US-European Relations*
Alton Frye, *Institute for Congress*
Norman Gall, *Brazil*
Leslie H. Gelb, *Security & Arms Control*
Robert K. German, *Soviet-Nordic Relations*
Richard Gilmore, *International Grain Trade*
James O. Goldsborough, *European Foreign Policies*

Thomas R. Graham, *International Trade*
Victor Gray, *Face-to-Face*
Catherine Gwin, *International Economic Institutions*
Thomas A. Halsted, *Arms Control Association*
Richard J. Harrington, *Face-to-Face*
Robert Hershman, *Media & Foreign Policy*
Vivian D. Hewitt, *Librarian*
Richard Holbrooke, *Foreign Policy Magazine*
William G. Hyland, *Soviet-American Relations*
Josef Joffe, *US-European Relations*
Robert H. Johnson, *US Conceptions of Soviet Threat*
Jonathan L. Kandell, *Latin America*
Richard J. Kessler, *US-Philippine Relations*
William H. Kincade, *Emerging Technology & Arms Control*
Susan M. Kling, *Face-to-Face*
Yoshihisa Komori, *US-Japanese Relations*
Steven P. Kramer, *Face-to-Face*
Michael Krepon, *Verification, Compliance & Arms Control*
Anthony Lake, *Rhodesia*
David Lascelles, *Bank-Government Relationships*
Robert Leiken, *Central America*
William H. Lewis,*I nternational Refugees*
Victor H. Li, *US-China Relations*
Karin M. Lissakers, *Banking & Foreign Policy*
Kenneth Longmyer, *Black Americans & US Foreign Policy*
Nicholas S. Ludington, *Turkey & the Western Alliance*
Charles Maechling, Jr., *Political / Legal Issues*
Christopher J. Makins, *Western Europe*
Alex W. Maldonado, *US-Puerto Rican Relations*
Raul S. Manglapus, *Japan & Southeast Asia*
Murrey Marder, *US-Soviet Relations*
Benjamin Martin, *Spanish Labor*
Michael H. C. McDowell, *Northern Ireland*

Donald F. McHenry, *Micronesia*
George Moffett, *Consensus & Foreign Policy*
Roger Morris, *The Sahel*
Edward Mortimer,*P olitical Impact of Islam*
Andrew Nagorski, *East-West Relations*
Joseph S. Nye, *Security & Arms Control*
Robert B. Oakley, *International Terrorism*
J. Daniel O'Flaherty, *Caribbean; South Africa*
Marvin Ott, *Japan-Middle East; Japan-US Technology Issues*
Charles D. Paolillo, *Foreign Aid & Congress*
Clyde V. Prestowitz, Jr., *International Competitiveness & Trade*
Robert M. Pringle, *Indonesia & the Philippines*
Mian Quadrud-Din, *North-South Issues*
Kevin F.F. Quigley, *Economic Sanctions*
Ze'ev Schiff, *Israel's Security Policies*
Jeffrey J. Schott, *Trade in Services*
Gebhard Schweigler, *US-European Relations*
Herbert Scoville, Jr., *Arms Control*
Deborah Shapley, *Antarctica*
Harry Shaw, *Security Assistance in US Foreign Policy*
Terri Shaw, *Central America*
Jack Shepherd, *US Food Aid to Africa*
S. Nihal Singh, *Indo-Soviet Relations*
Wayne S. Smith, *US-Cuban Relations*
James W. Spain, *The Eastern Mediterranean*
Ronald Steel, *US Alliances & Commitments*
Uwe Stehr, *Conventional Arms Control*
Ben S. Stephansky, *Latin America*
Robert Stephens, *Persian Gulf*
Laurence Stern, *Cyprus*
Paula Stern, *US Trade Policy*
William Stivers, *The US & the Persian Gulf*
Peter B. Swiers, *Face-to-Face*
Milan Svec, *East Europe & US-Soviet Relations*

Michael S. Teitelbaum, *Immigration & Foreign Policy*
Yvonne F. Thayer, *Face-to-Face*
W. Scott Thompson *Security & Development in the Third World*
John H. Trattner, *Government, Press & Foreign Policy*
Sanford J. Ungar, *Foreign Policy Magazine*
Brian Van Arkadie, *West Bank & Gaza Strip Economies*
Christopher Van Hollen, *Persian Gulf & Southwest Asia*
Lannon Walker, *Conflicts in Africa*
Stephen M. Walt, *Radical Regimes*
David Webster, *International Communications*
Warren Weinstein, *UN & Human Rights*
G. Anthony Westell, *Canadian-US Economic Relations*
Robert E. White, *Central America*
Sharon P. Wilkinson, *Face-to-Face*
Eric Willenz, *European Social Peace & US Foreign Policy*
Mark Leon Wiznitzer, *Face-to-Face*
Robin B. Wright, *Religion & Third World Militancy*
Jose Zalaquett, *Human Rights & Authoritarian Governments*
Ralph Zacklin, *International Law*
Peter D. Zimmerman, *Arms Control & Strategic Defense*
Warren Zimmermann, *Europe's Future*

Appendix C

Estimated Impacts on U.S. Gross National Product (GNP) and Employment Resulting from a U.S. Embargo on South African Platinum—Group Metal Supplies

Open File Report, 54-88, U.S. Bureau of Mines

Division of Policy Analysis

Marilyn Biviano
Stan Miller
George Swisko

September 1988

Executive Summary

This analysis was conducted in response to concerns raised by the Chairman of the Energy and Commerce Committee of the House of Representatives regarding the potential impacts on automobile production, GNP and employment resulting from embargoing South African supplies of the platinum-group metals, platinum and rhodium. This analysis should be considered an addendum to the recently release study in which the direct economic costs[1] of a U.S. embargo on selected South African strategic and critical materials are estimated. The estimated GNP and employment impacts result when a mineral shortage reduces domestic industrial production and are in addition to the direct costs estimated in the earlier study.

The direct cost to this nation resulting from a decision to embargo six South African strategic and critical minerals was estimated at $1.85 billion per year during the 1988-1992 time frame of the study. The estimated direct costs include the costs to U.S. consumers resulting from higher strategic mineral prices, lower mineral consumption, and the cost of developing higher cost domestic mineral resources. A large proportion of the costs result from the shortage of the two metals: platinum and rhodium. The average direct annual cost of embargoing is estimated at about $1.4 billion for platinum and $384 million for rhodium.[2]

The primary domestic application of platinum and rhodium is in emission control systems for automobiles, accounting for over two-thirds of U.S. consumption of these two metals in 1987. Platinum and rhodium are used in emission control systems in order to meet the Clean Air Act control requirements for carbon monoxide, hydrocarbons, and nitrous oxides. Studies indicate that there are no substitutes for platinum and rhodium in this applica-

---

[1]Biviano, Marilyn; Gillette, Richard; and Smith, Pamela, Bureau of Mines, "Estimated Direct Economic Impacts of a U.S. Embargo on Strategic and Critical Minerals Produced in South Africa," January 1988, OFR 19-88.

[2]Biviano, Marilyn; Gillette, Richard; and Smith, Pamela, Bureau of Mines, Ibid, pp ES-1, ES-3.

tion nor could the development of promising alternatives be expected before 1995.

During the 5-year time frame of the study, estimated available U.S. supply without South African platinum and rhodium supplies would be insufficient to meet U.S. platinum and rhodium industrial consumption requirements. The estimated platinum shortage would not be as severe and no reduction in U.S. automobile production would be expected to result from embargoing platinum.

Reduced automobile production and substantial GNP and employment losses, however, are estimated to result from embargoing South African rhodium supplies. Assuming no change in the current emission control requirements of the Clean Air Act, and that the United States does not import South African rhodium as a metal directly or indirectly, even as an ingredient in manufactured products, an impact on the level of domestic automobile production would be expected, resulting in estimated GNP losses of $61 billion. Losses estimated at $34 billion would occur in the second year of the embargo and $27 billion in the third year. GNP losses are estimated to average $12 billion annually from 1988-1992 (Table 1).

These national economic impact estimates include losses to automobile manufacturers, automobile dealerships, the transportation and wholesale industries which sell and deliver the automobiles to the dealerships, all the

Table 1

Estimates of Average Annual Direct Economic Costs, GNP Losses and Employment Losses of a U.S. Embargo of South African Rhodium

Direct Cost to Rhodium Consumers Million $1987	Gross National Product Losses Million $1987	Employment Losses Average Number of Jobs per Annum
384	12,000	206,000

other industries which directly and indirectly sell goods
and services to these industries, and the associated reduced spending by employees in these sectors.

Estimated U.S. employment losses associated with
the GNP losses would be about 572 thousand jobs in the
second year of the embargo and 458 thousand jobs in the
third year, and average 206 thousand jobs per year during
1988-1992. About 16 percent of the estimated employment
loss would be in the manufacture of motor vehicles and
parts, 24 percent in other manufacturing industries such
as steel, tires, and glass, 30 percent in wholesale and retail
trade, and the remaining 30 percent in other non-manufacturing sectors such as agriculture, mining, services and
construction.

Introduction

This analysis was conducted in response to concerns
raised by the Chairman of the Energy and Commerce
Committee of the House of Representatives regarding the
potential impacts on automobile production, Gross National Product (GNP) and employment resulting from
embargoing South African supplies of the platinum-group
metals (PGM's), platinum and rhodium. This analysis
should be considered an addendum to the recently released study[1] in which the direct economic costs of a U.S.
embargo on selected South African strategic and critical
materials were estimated. The estimated GNP and employment impacts result when a mineral shortage reduces
the level of domestic industrial production and are in
addition to the direct costs estimated in the earlier study.

The direct cost to this nation resulting from a decision

---

[1]Biviano, Marilyn; Gillette, Richard; and Smith, Pamela, Bureau of
Mines, "Estimated Direct Economic Impacts of a U.S. Import Embargo
on Strategic and Critical Minerals Produced in South Africa, January
1988, OFR 19-88.

to embargo six South African strategic and critical minerals—including the PGM's, chromium, manganese, rutile (titanium source materials), vanadium and cobalt—is estimated at $1.85 billion per year during the 1988-1992 time frame of the study. The estimated direct costs include the costs to U.S. consumers resulting from higher strategic mineral prices, lower mineral consumption, and the cost of developing higher cost domestic mineral resources. A large proportion of the costs would result from the shortage of two of the PGM's, platinum and rhodium. The average direct annual cost of embargoing is estimated at about $1.4 billion for platinum and $384 million for rhodium.[2]

The major assumptions underlying the South African minerals embargo economic analysis are presented in Table 1.1.

Table 1.1

Major Assumptions of Embargo Analysis

• A U.S. embargo of South African strategic and critical minerals begins in 1988 and continues indefinitely. The analytical time frame of the embargo economic impact analyses is 1988-1992.

• South African minerals are not supplied to the United States during the embargo, either directly or indirectly, even as ingredients in manufactured products.

• The U.S. embargo is unilateral—no other countries join the embargo.

• Trade patterns are adjustable. All non-South African production is available to the United States at a price, excepting material that is produced and consumed within the Soviet Bloc.

• Soviet sales to the world market are maintained during the embargo, and all of these supplies are made available to the United States.

• The Clean Air Act automobile emission control requirements are maintained throughout the embargo.

• Releases of strategic and critical minerals from the National Defense Stockpile, additions to supply resulting from government-sponsored domestic production incentives, and technological changes affecting mineral supply and demand are not considered.

Analysis of GNP and Employment Impacts

Estimated available U.S. supply for two of the South African minerals analyzed, platinum and rhodium, would be insufficient to meet U.S. requirements. U.S. inventories, secondary production and non-South African production would be insufficient to meet U.S. requirements during two or more years of the 5-year study time frame. The estimated shortage would not be as severe in the case of platinum, and no constraint on U.S. industrial production is estimated to result from the U.S. embargo.

Platinum—The primary industrial application of platinum is in the production of automotive catalytic converters. Over two-thirds of 1987 domestic platinum consumption was in this application. The remaining industrial applications account for about one-third of U.S. consumption. Petroleum refining and chemical produc-

---

[3]Office of Technology Assessments, "Strategic Materials: Technologies to Reduce U.S. Import Vulnerability," Washington, DC, 1985, pp 243-245.

[4]Johnson Matthey Public Limited Company, "Platinum 1987," 1987, London, England, p 57.

[5]Feichtinger, F., A. Lammer, and Riess, M., "Platinum: The View From South Africa," *Mining Engineering*, V. 40, No. 2, February 1988, pp 91-92.

tion accounted for 10 percent of U.S. consumption in 1987; electronics, including electrical circuits; thermocouples; and electrical contacts (7 percent); glass and jewelry (2 percent); and dental and medical uses (2 percent).

There are no substitutes for the PGM's in auto catalytic converters.[3,4,5] The PGM's, platinum palladium, and rhodium are required to meet current U.S. automobile emission standards. Platinum, specifically, is required to meet the emission controls on carbon monoxide and hydrocarbons as prescribed by the Clean Air Act. In a major assessment of alternative technologies that could be used to reduce U.S. consumption of strategic and critical materials, the Office of Technology Assessment (OTA) concluded that "near-term (before 1995) alternatives to PGM use in the catalytic converter are not promising. Most currently developed alternatives would entail a major loss of fuel economy and/or a need to relax automotive emission standards." The OTA findings that there are no available substitutes either for the catalytic converter or for the PGM's used in catalytic converters nor could alternatives be developed by 1995 were confirmed by domestic catalytic converter and automobile producers at the onset of this analysis.[6] A recent analysis of substitutes for the PGM's extended the forecast that there are no alternatives to PGM's in automobile emission control to 1998.[7]

About 80 percent of the annual U.S. platinum requirements would be met during the 5-year study time

---

[6]In June of 1988, two major domestic catalytic converter producers, Englehard and Johnson Matthey, Inc. and the auto catalyst divisions of General Motors, Ford, and Chrysler were interviewed by the Policy Analysis Division regarding the substitutability of alternative materials for each of the platinum-group metals in catalytic converters and alternative technologies to the catalytic converter.

[7]Feichtinger, F., A. Lammer, and Riess, M., Ibid.

frame, assuming that all of the non-South African sources of platinum supply to market economy countries were exported to the United States at estimated premium U.S. prices, and that U.S. primary and secondary platinum production expanded to provide over one-third of domestic platinum requirements.

The estimated shortfall of platinum could be offset by reduced consumption in the non-automobile catalytic converter sectors. Substitutes are available in some of the electrical, catalytic, and glass applications.[8] Assuming feasible platinum substitution takes place where possible and platinum consumption in jewelry were eliminated, given an estimated six-fold increase in the U.S. platinum price during the South Africa embargo, no impact on U.S. automobile production should result from the South African embargo on platinum.

Rhodium—Assuming no change in the current emission control standards of the Clean Air Act, a decline in the level of automobile production and substantial GNP losses are estimated to result from embargoing South African rhodium supplies.

The primary application of rhodium is in the production of automotive catalytic converters. Over 70 percent of U.S. consumption is in this application, and there are no available substitutes. Rhodium is also used in the production of chemicals and electronics where substitution is also very limited.[9]

There are no substitutes for the PGM's in auto catalytic converters.[10, 11, 12] Rhodium is required in the produc-

---

[8]Loebenstein, J. Roger, Physical Scientist, Platinum-Group Metals Specialist, Bureau of Mines.

[9]Loebenstein, J. Roger, Ibid.

[10]Office of Technology Assessment, Ibid.

[11]Johnson Matthey Public Limited Company, Ibid.

[12]Feichtinger, F., A. Lammer, and Riess, M., Ibid.

tion of catalytic converters to meet Clean Air Act nitrous oxides (NOX) emission control standards. Further, development of substitutes or alternative technologies in this application could not be expected before 1995 (see platinum analysis). Assuming that no South African rhodium were supplied to the United States during the embargo, all of the non-South African sources of supply to market economy countries were exported to the United States, and that all Soviet exports to market economy countries were shipped to the United States, over one-third of U.S. rhodium requirements would not be met in two years of the 5-year study time frame. Further, assuming no rhodium consumption in non-auto catalyst applications, a minimum shortfall of 25 percent of rhodium requirements in the auto catalyst sector is estimated in the second year of the embargo, and a minimum of about 20 percent of requirements in the third years.

In order to maintain the assumed effective embargo of South African minerals, imports of catalytic converters containing South African rhodium are assumed to be also embargoed. Further, because all of the non-South African rhodium supplies have been imported at the premium U.S. rhodium prices (in this analysis), all catalytic converters manufactured abroad would be embargoed since, by inference, they contain South African rhodium.

The rhodium shortfall would reduce both catalytic converter production and automobile production. A reduction of 2.9 million catalytic converters is estimated to

---

[13]The estimated rhodium shortage to the auto sector in the second year of the embargo is about 17.2 thousand ounces. Based on the Bureau of Mines platinum-group metals industrial consumers survey, about .006 ounces of rhodium are needed to produce one catalytic converter. Thus, it is estimated that as a result of the 17.2 thousand ounce rhodium shortage in the automobile industry, 2.9 million catalytic converters will not be produced domestically (17,200 ounces/.006 ounces per catalytic converters = 2.9 million catalytic converters.

result from the 25 percent rhodium shortage.[13] About 80 percent of catalytic converters[14] are used in the production of new vehicles; the remainder are used as replacement parts. Assuming no U.S. imports of South African rhodium either as rhodium or in catalytic converters manufactured abroad, and no relaxation in the automobile emission standards affecting rhodium consumption, automobile (includes light trucks) production is estimated to decline by 2.3 million vehicles[15] in the second year of the embargo.

In the third year of the embargo, automobile production is estimated to decline by about 1.8 million vehicles as a result of the estimated 20 percent decline in catalytic converters produced.

Impact on GNP and Employment—The total estimated GNP losses during a 5-year embargo resulting from reduced automobile production have been developed using interindustry analysis. As a result of the 2.3 million U.S. automobile vehicle production decline, estimated GNP losses would be $61 billion, with $34 billion occurring in the second year of the embargo and $27 billion in the third year. GNP losses would average $12 billion annually from 1988-1992 (Table 1).[16] These estimates include losses to automobile manufacturers, automobile dealerships, the transportation and wholesale industries which sell and deliver the automobiles to the dealerships, all the

---

[14]1982 Census of Manufactures, Industry Series Report MC82-I-37A, Motor Vehicles and Equipment. Table 6a, Product and Product Classes—Quantity and Value by all producers 1982 and 1977, page 37a-19.

[15]Estimated catalytic converter production decline: 2.9 million catalytic converters times percent of catalytic converters used in new cars: 80 percent = 2.3 million catalytic converters.

[16]GNP and employment impacts estimated by George Swisko, economist, Bureau of Mines using the Forest Service's IMPLAN Input-Output Model.

other industries which directly and indirectly sell goods and services to these industries, and the associated reduced spending by employees in these sectors.

Estimated U.S. employment losses associated with the GNP losses would be about 572 thousand jobs in the second year of the embargo and 458 thousand jobs in the third year, averaging 206 thousand jobs per year during 1988-1992. About 16 percent of the estimated employment loss would occur in the manufacture of motor vehicles and parts, 24 percent in other manufacturing industries such as steel, tires, and glass, 30 percent in wholesale and retail trade, and the remaining 30 percent in other non-manufacturing sectors such as agriculture, mining, services and construction (Table 1.2).

Table 1.2

Estimates of Average Annual Employment Losses of a U.S. Embargo of South African Rhodium in Major Sectors of the Economy

Industry	Employment losses
Manufacturing	
Motor Vehicles and Parts	33,000
Other	49,000
Non-manufacturing	
Wholesale and Retail Trade	62,000
Other	62,000
	206,000

Appendix D

Estimated Direct Economic Impacts of a U.S. Import Embargo on Strategic and Critical Minerals Produced in South Africa

Open File Report, 19-88, U.S. Bureau of Mines

Marilyn Biviano
Richard Gillette
Pamela Smith

January 1988

Executive Summary

Major Findings

1. The direct economic costs to this nation resulting from a decision to embargo South African[1] strategic and critical minerals imports are estimated at $1.85 billion per

year.[1,2,3] About 94 percent of these estimated costs are for two platinum-group metals (PGM's), platinum and rhodium. The estimated costs of a 5-year embargo beginning in 1988 for the strategic and critical minerals analyzed are presented in Table 1.[4]

2. There are sufficient alternative world sources to South Africa for manganese, chromium, palladium, titanium, and vanadium to meet U.S. industrial demand in the event of an embargo.

3. Alternative world sources to South Africa for platinum and rhodium cannot meet U.S. industrial demand. Non-South African world supply sources can meet about 40 percent of domestic platinum consumption requirements and 50 percent of rhodium requirements.

4. As a result of the increase in prices for platinum and rhodium during the embargo, expansion of domestic platinum-group metals mining and secondary production is expected. During a five-year embargo, domestic primary and secondary production expand and together satisfy about one-third of U.S. platinum requirements, one-third of U.S. rhodium requirements, and over one-half of domestic palladium requirements.

---

[1]South Africa(n) is used herein to refer to the Republic of South Africa.

[2]The direct economic costs estimated include the (1) increased cost of the material imported at the higher embargo price, lower mineral consumption, and the cost of developing low-grade domestic ores or high-cost secondary recovery, or (2) estimated trade pattern adjustment costs. National or gross national product (GNP) impacts have not been estimated in this study. If a material shortage exists and constrains production, national or GNP impacts could be expected. Losses in GNP represent the real constraints on domestic industrial production resulting from raw material shortages.

[3]Releases of strategic and critical minerals from the National Defense Stockpile, additions to supply resulting from domestic production incentives, and technological changes affecting the supply and demand for a mineral have not been considered in this analysis.

5. As a result of the embargo, dependence on the Soviet Union for the platinum-group metals is estimated to increase substantially. U.S. dependence on the Soviet Union for platinum increases from 3 to 30 percent of consumption requirements, rhodium dependency doubles from one-third to as high as two-thirds, and palladium increases from 33 percent to as high as 60 percent of total consumption requirements. Further, because the Soviet Union is a major producer of chromium, manganese, and vanadium, U.S. dependence on the Soviet Union for these minerals may also increase as a result of an embargo on South African minerals.

Study Background and Scope

The Comprehensive Anti-Apartheid Act of 1986 prohibits U.S. imports of products produced, manufactured, marketed or exported by South African parastatal organizations.[5] Certain strategic and critical minerals have been exempt from that ban. Section 501(c) of the Act introduces additional measures that could be undertaken by the United States, including the prohibition of strategic and critical material imports from South Africa. To assist the President and the Congress in determining the national

---

[4]If South African production is disrupted (rather than a unilateral U.S. embargo imposed), South African supplies are unavailable to any world consumer. In this case, unless there is sufficient excess world production capacity to cover the lost South African production, a trade pattern adjustment will not offset the disrupted production and economic impacts will be greater than in the case of a U.S. embargo.

The direct economic costs to the United States of disrupted South African chromium and manganese production have been estimated in a Bureau of Mines study "South Africa and Critical Materials" (OFR 76-86). The direct cost to the United States of a 3-year disruption of chromium was estimated at $3.6 billion, and manganese at $1 billion.

[5]A parastatal organization is defined as a corporation or partnership owned, controlled, or subsidized by the government of South Africa.

Table 1

**Estimated Direct Economic Cost of an Embargo
on South African Strategic and Critical Minerals
(Million 1987 Dollars)**

	Average Annual Cost	Cumulative Embargo Cost 1988-1992
Platinum Group Metals		
Platinum	1,355	6,775
Rhodium	384	1,920
Palladium	7	35
Chromium	30	150
Manganese	31	155
Titanium (Rutile)	32	160
Vanadium	7	35
Cobalt[1]	4	20
Total	1,850	9,250

[1]Upper end of range of estimated costs of exporting Zairian cobalt to the United States using non-South African transportation.

implications of such a prohibition, at the request of the Department of State, the direct costs to this nation resulting from a U.S. embargo on South African strategic and critical minerals have been assessed by the Bureau of Mines.

The minerals or mineral groups produced by (or transported for export through) South Africa which are included in this assessment include: platinum, palladium, and rhodium of the platinum-group metals; chromium (including ferrochrome); manganese (all forms); vanadium (including ferrovanadium); titanium source materials, including rutile and rutile substitutes (titaniferous slag); and cobalt (which is transported through South Africa.

Introduction

Under Section 303 of the Comprehensive Anti-Apartheid Act of 1986 (P.L. 99-440) U.S. imports of products produced, manufactured, marketed or exported by South African parastatal organizations are prohibited. Strategic and critical minerals for which the President has certified to the Congress are essential for the economy or defense, and which are unavailable from reliable and secure suppliers, are exempt from this ban. Section 501(c) of the Act, however, introduces additional measures that could be undertaken, including the prohibition of strategic and critical material imports from South Africa.

To assist the President and the Congress in determining the national implications of such a prohibition, at the request of the Department of State, the direct costs to this nation resulting from a U.S. embargo on South African strategic and critical minerals have been assessed by the Bureau of Mines. The minerals included in this analysis are:

• Platinum, palladium and rhodium of the platinum-group metals
  • Chromium (all forms of contained chromium)
  • Manganese (all forms of contained manganese)
  • Vanadium
  • Titanium (rutile and rutile substitutes)
  • Cobalt (that is transported through South Africa for export)

South Africa as a Supplier of Strategic and Critical Minerals

The Republic of South Africa is a major world producer of strategic and critical minerals, including the

Table 1.1

South Africa as a World Supplier of Selected Strategic and Cricital Minerals 1985-1986, Average (Percent)

	South Africa/ World Mine Production	South Africa/ MEC Mine Production	South Africa/ World Reserve Base
Platinum-Group Metals	48	90	90
Chromium	34	52	84
Manganese	15	29	71
Titanium (Rutile)	31	31	17
Vanadium	40	93	47
Cobalt	<1		NA

Sources: Mineral Commodity Summaries 1987 and Minerals Yearbook 1986 preprints

platinum-group metals, chromium, manganese, vanadium, and rutile (and rutile substitutes). In fact, South Africa is the largest or second largest producer of these minerals in the world. From 1985 through 1986, South Africa contributed an estimated 15 to 49 percent of the total world product of these minerals (Table 1.1). Omitting the production of the Soviet Union, another major world producer, and other centrally planned economies, South Africa produced 29 to 93 percent of the world total in those years.

In terms of long-term rather than current supply, South Africa has from 17 to 90 percent of the world reserve base for these minerals.

South Africa produces only a small quantity of cobalt as a byproduct of its platinum-group metal (PGM) production. However, cobalt produced in Zaire, which contributed 57 percent of the total world cobalt production from 1985 through 1986, is shipped on South African rail to port for export.

The United States relies heavily on imports for all of

Table 1.2

**U.S. Import Dependence for Selected Strategic
and Critical Minerals from South Africa, 1985-1986
Average (Percent)**

	U.S. Import Reliance	Imports from South Africa/Total U.S. Imports
Platinum-Group Metals	95	60
Chromium	79	76
Manganese	100	29
Titainium (Rutile)	78	54
Vanadium	54	58
Cobalt	85	<1

Sources: Mineral Commodity Summaries 1987 and Minerals Yearbook
    1986 preprints.

these minerals. From 1985 through 1986, imports provided from 54 to 100 percent of our domestic requirements for the platinum-group metals, manganese, chromium and cobalt (Table 1.2). The United States depends on imports to meet most of its chromium and PGM requirements and about one-half of these imports come from South Africa.

Embargo Analysis

The impacts of a U.S. embargo on these strategic and critical materials greatly depend on whether:

1. Other countries also embargo South African strategic and critical minerals.

2. The embargo is effective, i.e., South African minerals are not exported to the United States either directly of transshipped through another country and then exported to the United States.

3. There are sufficient alternative world suppliers to

meet any domestic shortfall resulting from this action.

In regard to the first two considerations, it is assumed in this analysis that the embargo is unilateral (no other countries embargo South African minerals), and that the United States does not import South African minerals directly of indirectly. The embargo is assumed to be effective in order to provide Congress and the President with an upper bound on the estimated direct costs of a decision to embargo South African strategic and critical minerals.

The impacts of a unilateral, effective embargo depend greatly on whether there are sufficient alternative world suppliers to meet any shortfall resulting from this action. The major assumptions used in the embargo analysis are presented in Table 1.3.

Table 1.3

Major Assumptions of Embargo Analysis

• The analytic time frame of the embargo impact analysis is 1988-1992.

• A U.S. import embargo of South African strategic and critical minerals begins in 1988 and continues indefinitely.

• The United States does not import strategic and critical minerals that were mined in, refined in, or transported through South Africa. In essence the embargo creates a second world mineral market consisting of U.S. demand and non-South African supply of the embargoed materials from market economy and centrally planned economy countries.

• Trade patterns of the world market may adjust during the embargo, i.e., non-South African supplies of the embargoed materials that were formerly exported to countries other than the United States can be made available to this country.

• Estimated trade adjustment costs of the U.S. embargo will be borne by U.S. consumers.

• Releases of strategic and critical minerals from
the National Defense Stockpile, additions to supply
resulting from domestic production incentives, and
technological changes affecting mineral supply and
demand will not be considered.

Analytical Approach

The analytical approach which estimates the direct
economic impacts of a U.S. import embargo on the South
African strategic and critical minerals involves an initial
assessment of whether available supplies from non-South
African sources, including net exports by centrally planned
economies, and supplies made available by secondary
recovery, equals or exceeds U.S. consumption requirements during the 1988-1992 impact period. If there are
sufficient alternative sources, the estimated embargo costs
are the trade adjustment costs. If there are not sufficient
alternative sources to South Africa to satisfy U.S. industrial demand, then the direct economic costs are estimated
using a market model. The approach for estimating costs
under these alternative cases is presented below. In addition to the estimated costs, there could be implications for
the security of U.S. supplies in both cases because of
increased U.S. dependency on the Soviet Bloc for strategic
and critical minerals.[6]

Sufficient Non-South African U.S. Supplies

Assuming a total constraint on South African exports
to the United States, and that each producer sells his

---

[6]An anlysis of the security of alternative sources is beyond the scope
of this study. The Department of Commerce is monitoring and reporting
on U.S. dependency on the Soviet Bloc for strategic and critical materials (U.S. Department of Commerce Section 502(b)(2) Report, Public
Law 99-440," April 1987).

supply to the highest bidder, the world trade flows of the affected mineral will be adjusted after the embargo and non-South African mineral exports will be sold to U.S. consumers to offset the embargoed South African imports.

In this case, the costs of the embargo can be viewed as the adjustment fee, or premium, that U.S. consumers would need to offer non-south African producers to obtain the needed supplies. The premium would include the costs associated with such trade adjustments including the costs of abrogating existing contractual arrangements, the costs of altering logistical systems, any additional transportation costs involved in the rearrangement of international trade flows, the substitution of higher priced materials, and increased production from higher cost in-place sources. A higher premium could be expected where major changes to well established trade patterns are required, or increases in production by alternative sources is required.

Procedures for Trade Pattern Impact Estimation

Based on Bureau of Mines information and expertise, trade adjustment costs resulting from an effective embargo have been estimated. This process involved an assessment and quantification of:

1. Alternative world sources of supply and information on the form and quality of these source materials.

2. World production capacities and capacity utilization rates.

3. Production costs of available alternative sources.

4. The use of expert judgment of the commodity and foreign data specialists of the Bureau of Mines. The adjustment fee, a premium paid by U.S. consumers, was estimated as a percentage of the base case or base year price of the commodity and ranged from 10 to 50 percent

higher than the current price for each year of the embargo for the minerals studied.

The cost of embargoing cobalt that is exported from central Africa through South Africa was estimated as the incremental transportation costs involved in using an alternative transportation route.

U.S. Supply-Demand Balance

If U.S. demand exceeds available non-South African supplies and supplies from U.S. secondary recovery, a U.S. supply shortfall would result, and direct economic costs to U.S. consumers could be expected in terms of higher prices and reduced supplies.

Procedures for Supply-Demand Imbalance Impact Estimation

The direct economic cost of supply-demand imbalances are quantitatively estimated using formal world market analytical systems. This cost estimate has three components. The first component is the increased cost of material imported at the higher price brought on by a disruption of normal mineral supplies (Area 1 in Figure 1.1). The second component is termed the deadweight loss, and measures the costs of reduced consumption or the necessity to use substitute materials when the minerals are at the higher, embargo prices (Area 2 in Figure 1.1). The final social cost component is a measure of the real resources expended for the production of low-grade domestic ores or secondary recovery to increase U.S. supplies (Area 3 of Figure 1.1). Only the proportion of production costs that is in excess of normal costs from current world producers is counted as a direct economic cost.

National or gross national product (GNP) impacts have not been estimated in this study. If a material shortage exists and constrains production, national or the

Figure 1.1

U.S. Direct Economic Cost

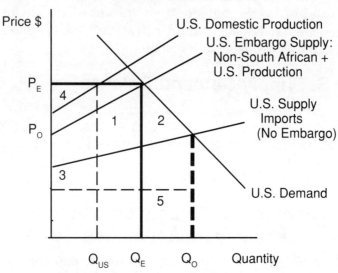

P$_E$: Embargo Price
P$_O$: Initial Price
Q$_E$: U.S. Consumption During Embargo
Q$_O$: U.S. Consumption—No Embargo
Q$_{US}$: U.S. Production

Area #1 = Transfer to non-South African suppliers after embargo
Area #2 = Net (deadweight) loss, consumers purchase less
Area #3 = Net loss as U.S. resources are diverted from more
          efficient uses to domestic production
Area #4 = Transfer from U.S. buyers of strategic minerals to U.S.
          producers
Area #5 = U.S. consumer spending diverted to other goods

GNP impacts could be expected. Losses in GNP represent the real constraints on domestic industrial production resulting from raw material shortages. For example, domestic industrial production and GNP are affected to the extent that U.S. platinum and rhodium shortages constrain domestic catalytic converter production, and in turn, domestic automobile production. In such a case, the costs to the economy could be expected to be greater than the estimated direct economic costs.

Mineral Analysis
Platinum-Group Metals

The platinum-group metals (PGM's) include platinum, palladium, rhodium, ruthenium, iridium, and osmium. The PGM's have certain extraordinary physical and chemical properties—refactoriness, chemical inertness and excellent catalytic activity. The United States consumed 2.2 million ounces of PGM's, on average, from 1984 through 1986. Three of the PGM's, platinum, palladium, and rhodium, constituted about 95 percent of domestic PGM consumption. These three PGM's are used in the production of automobile catalytic converters, by far the largest end use, which represented about 40 percent of domestic PGM consumption from 1984 through 1986. Domestic demand for PGM's in this end use has increased steadily because of legislated environmental emission standards. European and Japanese demand is also showing a steady increase because of their environmental legislation and regulation.

From 1983-1985, about 53 percent of United States PGM supplies, either directly or indirectly, came from South African, and about 10 percent came from the Soviet Union. Canada is the third leading United States supplier, providing about 7 percent of world supply in that three-year period. Other market economy countries provided about 20 percent of domestic PGM imports, but most of these PGM's were not mined in these countries. Less than 1 percent of world PGM mine production is contributed by other market economy countries. The remaining 10 percent of U.S. supply was provided by secondary recovery, primarily from catalytic converters.

The Stillwater Mine in Montana is the only producing U.S. PGM mine, and the only mine outside of South Africa that mines the platinum-group metals as primary products. PGM's are recovered as byproducts in other operations. The Stillwater Mine, which began producing in March of 1987 with an annual capacity of about 75,000 ounces of palladium and 25,000 ounces of platinum, could satisfy about 2.5 percent of annual domestic platinum consumption requirements.

About 90 percent of the estimated world's PGM's reserve base is located in South Africa. The Soviet Union has about 9.5 percent of the estimated world reserve base. The United States and Canada, together, have less than 1 percent. South Africa, the Soviet Union and Canada account for nearly all of the world's newly mined or primary PGM. South Africa is the leading source of supply to the Western world for the PGM's excepting palladium, and the Soviet Union is the leading supplier of palladium and the second largest supplier of the other PGM's.

Platinum

U.S. Supplies and Demands

In 1986, U.S. platinum demand was about 1 million troy ounces. Omitting the Soviet Bloc, U.S. demand was about 40 percent of the world total. Industrial uses comprised 82 percent and investment demand 18 percent of total domestic consumption. The primary industrial application of platinum is in the production of automotive catalytic converters, and about two-thirds of 1986 total domestic industrial consumption was used in this application. Platinum was also used in reforming catalysts to upgrade the octane rating of gasolines, and in the production of chemicals (11 percent) and electronics (11 percent). In 1986, directly and indirectly, the United States imported 86 percent of its supplies from South Africa. The remaining supplies were provided by Canada (5 percent), the Soviet Union (3 percent), other sources (1 percent) and U.S. secondary recovery (5 percent).

Outside the Soviet Bloc, there are insufficient alternative supply sources to South Africa to meet United States platinum metal requirements. In 1986, the total production of countries other than South Africa and the Soviet Union, including domestic primary and secondary production, could only satisfy about 40 percent of United States demand.

Embargo Analysis and Impact Estimation

An analytic system has been developed[7] and modified[8] to estimate the impacts of a South African platinum embargo by the United States. The analytic system includes the major non-South African producing (mining rather than refining) sources: Canada, other market economy countries (MEC's), and the Soviet Bloc nations.

If the United States could not import platinum that was mined in South Africa, either directly or through a third country, a major shortage could be expected with significant attendant direct economic costs.

Demand for platinum is relatively inelastic, i.e., a percent change in the price of platinum results in a much smaller percent change in platinum consumption. In fact, because emission control is legislated, auto catalyst platinum demand is determined primarily by automobile

---

[7]Resource Strategies, Inc., *Platinum Supply and Demand Model*, 1986.

[8]John Bennett, Economist, Bureau of Mines and J. Roger Loebenstein, Platinum Group Metals Specialist, Bureau of Mines were responsible for modification of the system.

production, not the price of platinum and rhodium. Thus, consumption of platinum in the auto catalyst sector is maintained throughout the embargo. Total annual consumption of platinum, however, is 21 percent lower, on average than the baseline projection.

The average price of platinum increases by 466 percent over the projected baseline prices during the five-year period. The maximum price increase is about six times the baseline project (see page 59).

Estimated Impacts

The following impacts could be expected as a result of a U.S. embargo on South African platinum supplies:

1. The direct economic cost to the United States is estimated to average $1.36 billion annually during impact period, or $6.77 billion cumulatively for the 1988-1992 period (Table 1 and Table 1.4). About 76 percent of the estimated cost consists of increased payments to foreign producers resulting from the higher prices paid for platinum during the embargo. In addition, a modest cost increment results from reduced consumption of platinum (the deadweight loss), and from the higher cost of domestic production.

2. U.S. imports increase from non-South African in-place sources, the Soviet Union and Canada.

3. As a result of the sustained high platinum prices occurring during the embargo, new and expanded sources of supply for U.S. consumers come on-line in the United States (primary and secondary), Australia, and Canada. Domestic mine production from platinum-palladium resources and secondary recovery of platinum from auto catalysts increases to satisfy about one-third of domestic platinum requirements.

4. U.S. dependence on the Soviet Union for platinum is estimated to increase significantly. In 1987 Soviet platinum supplies provided 3 percent of U.S. consumption

Table 1.4

Estimated Direct Economic Cost of a
U.S. Embargo on South African Platinum
(Million 1987 Dollars)

	Average Annual Cost	5-Year Cumulative Embargo Cost
Platinum Group Metals		
Platinum	1,355	6,775

requirements. Under the embargo, Soviet supplies of platinum that were formerly sold to Japan and Europe are sold to the United States because of the higher U.S. platinum price and provide 30 percent of domestic consumption requirements.

Rhodium

U.S. Supplies and Demand

U.S. consumption of rhodium was about 100 thousand ounces in 1986. Omitting the Soviet Union and other centrally planned economies, U.S. consumption was almost one-half of the Western world total. The primary application of rhodium is in the production of automotive catalytic converters. Over 70 percent of U.S. consumption (93 thousand ounces in 1986) was used in this application in 1986. Rhodium demand is increasing worldwide as emission control requirements are placed on nitrous oxide emission, and as the control requirements are applied to a larger fleet of vehicles. Rhodium is also used in the production of chemicals, primarily nitric acid (5 percent), and in electronics (8 percent).

Rhodium is a very rare metal. South Africa recovers rhodium from its platinum ores, with a platinum-to-rhodium recovery ratio ranging from 1-to-20 to 1-to-15. Rhodium is also recovered as a byproduct of nickel production in Canada, and from copper-nickel production in the Soviet Union. Omitting the Soviet Union, world supply of rhodium is estimated at 212 thousand troy ounces in 1986. In 1986, South Africa provided about 53 percent of Western world supply, the Soviet Union 38 percent, Canada 5 percent, and secondary recovery 5 percent.

There are insufficient non-South African rhodium supplies to meet U.S. demand. Omitting South Africa, market economy countries produced 11 thousand troy ounces in 1986, less than 12 percent of U.S. consumption that year. Soviet Union sales to the West totaled 80 thousand ounces, but this was abnormally high, and it is believed to largely reflect a drawn down of producer stocks. From 1981-1986, Soviet Union sales to the West averaged 43,000 ounces annually. Assuming normal levels of Soviet sales to the West and that the remaining non-South African supplies are made available to the United States, a domestic supply shortfall of about 50 thousand ounces would result, which is equivalent to 54 percent of U.S. consumption in 1986.

Embargo Analysis and Impact Estimation

An analytical system has been developed[9] and modified[10] to estimate the impacts of a South African rhodium embargo on the United States. The rhodium model is to a large extent dependent on the platinum model because rhodium is a byproduct of platinum, and because of the close relationship between platinum and rhodium consumption in auto catalysts and in other industrial uses. The U.S. supply for rhodium under an embargo is modeled for the major non-South African producing (mining rather

---

[9]Resource Strategies, Inc., Platinum Supply and Demand Model, 1986.

[10]John Bennett, Economist, Bureau of Mines and J. Roger Loebenstein, Platinum Group Metals Specialist, Bureau of Mines were resopnsible for the modifications.

than refining) countries. These countries include Canada, other market economy countries (MEC's), and the Soviet Bloc. U.S. demand is modeled for auto catalysts and other industrial end uses.

If the United States could not import rhodium that was mined in South Africa, either directly or through a third country, a major domestic shortage could be expected. There are no domestic primary sources, and domestic secondary recovery is very limited. In the event of an embargo, the primary alternative source is the Soviet Union. Expansion of recycling is more limited in the case of rhodium than platinum. Rhodium-containing auto catalysts (three-way catalysts) have only been used since 1981; platinum-palladium auto catalysts have been used since 1974.

Because rhodium is used in auto catalysts and other industry catalysts for its superior catalytic properties, and because the quantities and respective value of rhodium used in these applications is very small, demand for rhodium is extremely inelastic, i.e., demand is relatively insensitive to price changes.[11]

As a result of the embargo there are insufficient available world supplies to meet domestic demand in the second and third years of the embargo. Consumption decreases can be expected in both auto catalysts and other industrial applications and may result in impacts on domestic industrial production. A decrease of 33 percent from the baseline consumption projection would result in the second year and 29 percent in the third year. The price of rhodium increases by an average of 824 percent over baseline price project during the five-year period, and the maximum price increase is about 10 times the baseline projection (see page 60).

---

[11]At $1,200 per troy ounce, about $7.20 of rhodium is contained in a catalytic converter.

Estimated Impacts

The following impacts could be expected as a result of an embargo on South African platinum supplies:

1. The direct economic cost to the United States from an embargo on South African rhodium imports is estimated to average $384 million annually during the five-year period, or $1.9 billion cumulatively (Table 1 and Table 1.5). About 83 percent of this cost results from increased transfers to foreigners because of the higher prices paid for rhodium during the embargo. The remaining 17 percent of the costs incurred result from reduced rhodium consumption (deadweight loss). No real resource costs are estimated since there will be no domestic rhodium production, and only modest increases in secondary recovery will occur during the embargo because of the limited stock of rhodium-containing catalytic converters.

2. U.S. imports increase from non-South African in-place sources, the Soviet Union and Canada.

3. As a result of the sustained high platinum prices occurring during the embargo, Canadian primary and U.S. secondary production would increase. Currently, rhodium secondary recovery is insignificant. However, during the five-year embargo, domestic recovery increases to provide about one-third of our rhodium consumption requirements.

4. U.S. dependence on the Soviet Union is expected to increase. In 1987, Soviet imports satisfied 33 percent of our industrial consumption requirements for rhodium. Soviet imports are estimated to increase to 40,000 ounces, providing up to two-thirds of the available domestic supply during the embargo.

5. If substitutes are unavailable, the shortfall of rhodium supply could reduce domestic industrial production and national income.

Table 1.5

Estimated Direct Economic Cost of a
U.S. Embargo on South African Rhodium
(Million 1987 Dollars)

	Average Annual Cost	5-Year Cumulative Embargo Cost
Platinum Group Metals		
Rhodium	384	1,920

Palladium

U.S. Supplies and Demand

The United States consumes about 1 million ounces of palladium annually, about one-third of the Western world total (1983-1986). The primary domestic applications of palladium are in electronics and electrical equipment (30 percent), dental and medical supplies (38 percent), and in auto catalysts (16 percent).

South Africa is the leading supplier of palladium to the United States and the second largest producer after the Soviet Union. On average, from 1985 through 1986, South Africa provided 41 percent of U.S. palladium supplies, and produced about 30 percent of the total 1986 palladium Western world supply. The Soviet Union is the largest supplier to the Western market, supplying about 1.5 million ounces (48 percent of total supply) in 1986. Canada provided about 4 percent of Western supply, Australia and Zimbabwe about 2 percent, and secondary recovery 16 percent of supply.

The Stillwater Mine in Montana is the only producing U.S. PGM mine, and the only mine outside of South Africa that mines the platinum-group metals as primary products. PGM's are recovered as byproducts in other operations. The Stillwater Mine, which began producing in March of 1987 with an annual capacity of about 75,000 ounces of palladium and 25,000 ounces of platinum, could provide about 8 percent of domestic palladium consumption requirements.

Embargo Analysis and Estimated Impacts

Assuming non-South African Western world supplies are made available to the United States through adjustments in world trade, the loss in South African supplies could be offset by supplies from the recently developed domestic source, the increased domestic production and recycling of palladium induced by the expanded production of platinum and rhodium during the embargo, and by increases in the U.S. share of Western world palladium supplies, primarily from the Soviet Union.

During the embargo, domestic palladium recycling increases and provides from 20 percent to about 33 percent of domestic consumption requirements during the embargo. Spurred by the significant embargo price increase for platinum, domestic platinum-palladium mine production provides about 30 percent of domestic palladium requirements by the fourth year of the embargo. Together, domestic sources provide over one-half of domestic requirements by the third year of the embargo.

The remaining 40 to 70 percent of domestic palladium requirements would be met by imports from the alternative suppliers to South Africa, primarily the Soviet Union. While a shortage of palladium is not expected under this scenario, a trade adjustment cost would result, i.e., U.S. consumers would offer the Soviets, the Canadian and Zimbabwean producers a premium for their palladium supplies. Based on expert judgment, a modest premium estimated at 10 percent over the world price is required to obtain these palladium supplies.

Table 1.6

Estimated Direct Economic Cost of a
U.S. Embargo on South African Palladium
(Million 1987 Dollars)

	AverageAnnual Cost	5-Year Cumulative Embargo Cost
Platinum Group Metals		
Palladium	7	35

Estimated Impacts

The following impacts could be expected as a result of an embargo on South African palladium supplies:

1. Based on the 1987 estimated price of $130 per ounce, the average annual premium which would be paid by U.S. consumers for palladium, is estimated at $7 million, or $35 million during the five-year impact period (Table 1 and Table 1.6).

2. As a result of the premium that U.S. consumers are willing to pay non-South African in-place sources, U.S. imports increase from the Soviet Union, Canada and Zimbabwe.

3. As a result of the sustained high platinum and rhodium prices occurring during the embargo, increases in domestic platinum-palladium production and secondary recovery of platinum, rhodium and palladium from auto catalysts is expected. During a five-year embargo, domestic recovery increases to provide over one-half of our domestic palladium requirements.

4. U.S. dependence on the Soviet Union will increase. In 1987, Soviet imports satisfied 33 percent of our industrial consumption requirements for palladium. During the embargo Soviet supplies satisfy as much as 60 percent of domestic consumption requirements according to the analysis.

Recommended Sources

The following firms and people on this list are recommended because they have generally dealt fairly with the public in the past and are considered to be reliable. Check carefully, however, and be satisfied in your own mind before doing business with any of these companies or any other for that matter.

Platinum Coins and Bars

Blanchard and Company
2400 Jefferson Highway
New Orleans, LA 70161

Rhyne Precious Metals, Inc.
425 Pike St.
Seattle, WA 98101
Tel. (206) 623-6900

Platinum Stocks

Ron Loewen
Pacific International Securities, Inc.
1500 700 W. Georgia St.
Vancouver, B.C. V7Y 1G1
Tel. (604) 669-2174

Platinum Futures

Geldermann & Company
440 S. La Salle St.
Chicago, IL 60605
Tel. (312) 663-7500

Bibliography

A. Leiss. Apartheid and United Nations Collective Measures, *Carnegie Endowment for International Peace.*

Loosening South Africa's Logjam. *Christian Science Monitor,* May 25, 1989.

Pauline Baker. Testimony Before Senate Foreign Relations Committee. *Carnegie Endowment,* October 1, 1989.

Pauline Baker. The American Challenge in South Africa. *Current History.*

M. Posner and P., and P. Goldberg. *The Strategic Metal Investment Handbook, 1984.*

M. Curran. *Economic Framework for Platinum Group Metals Deposits in Canada,* September, 1989.

Platinum Group Metals—South Africa. *Department of Minerals and Energy Affairs, Republic of South Africa,* 1988.

Impalla Platinum; Ltd. Annual Report, 1988.

Rustenburg Platinum Ltd. Annual Report, 1988.

Madeleine Mines Ltd. Annual Report, 1988.

Overseas Platinum Corp. Annual Report, 1988.

U.S. Platinum, Inc. Annual Report, 1988.

American Platinum Ltd. Annual Report, 1988.

R. Maybury. Buy Platinum Now for Political Reasons. *World Market Perspective,* Vol. XXIII, No. 7.

A.B. Korelin & Associates. *U.S. Platinum Report.*

Martin C. Spring. *Platinum Newsletter,* 1988.

Johnson Matthey. *Report: Platinum—The Precious Metal,* 1988.

Tokyo Exchange Overtaking More on Platinum Trading, *Wall Street Journal,* November 28, 1988.

South Africa—Act of Exorcism. *Wall Street Journal,* February 5, 1990.

Old Fusion. *Discover,* January, 1990.

Mandela. *Time,* February 5, 1990.

Estimated Direct Economic Impact of Import Embargo. *U.S. Bureau of Mines*, OFR 19, 1988.

The Platinum Group Metals. *Mining Survey*, South Africa, 1987.

Johnson Matthey. *Platinum*, 1989.

Mineral Position of the United States. *Annual Report: Department of Interior*, 1988.

Platinum. *Research Magazine*, 1987.

Englehardt Corp., *Annual Review*, 1988.

Mineral Issues (South African & Critical materials). *U.S. Bureau of Mines*.

Estimated Impact on Gross National Product From U.S. Embargo. U.S. *Bureau of Mines*, OFR 54-88.

Cold Fusion—A Case History. *Skeptical Inquirer*, January, 1990.

Fusion Illusion. *Time*, May 3, 1989.

Platinum. *Energy, Mines and Resources Canada*, 1989.

Platinum. *Platinum Guild*, 1989.

Potentially Critical Materials. *U.S. Department of Interior*, OFR 28-88.

R. Lubenstein. Platinum Group Metals. *U.S. Bureau of Mines*.

T.S. Ary. Research 88. *U. S. Bureau of Mines*.

Platinum Demand to Exceed Supply. *Wall Street Journal*, March 17, 1988.

A. Day Platinum—The Silent Crisis. *Investment Analyst*, September, 1989.

A Bullion Coin Menagerie. *Metals in the News*, January, 1989.

D. Rosenthal. I'm Turning Bullish on Platinum. *Silver-Gold Report (Special Edition)*.

Cold Fusion Dead? Development to Watch, *Time*, January 15, 1990.

Index